THE BOOK OF

Incomes

$

THE BOOK OF

Incomes

$

Gerald Krefetz and Philip Gittelman

Holt, Rinehart and Winston
NEW YORK

First published in January 1982 by Holt, Rinehart and Winston, 383 Madison Avenue, New York, New York 10017.

Published simultaneously in Canada by Holt, Rinehart and Winston of Canada, Limited.

Library of Congress Cataloging in Publication Data

Krefetz, Gerald.
The book of incomes.

Includes index.
1. Wages—United States. 2. Vocational guidance—United States
3. Income—United States. 4. Investments—United States.
5. Cost and standard of living—United States. I. Gittelman, Philip. II. Title.
HD4975.K73 1981 331.2'973 81-47472
AACR2

ISBN Hardbound: 0 03 059 897 4
ISBN Paperback: 0 03 056 848 X
First Edition

Designer: Robert Bull
Printed in the United States of America
10 9 8 7 6 5 4 3 2 1

CONTENTS

FOREWORD

Very few pieces of information are more avidly sought after than what people are paid, what they earn for a living. It is the first thing a new worker wants to know, and the last piece of data required for Social Security benefits.

Pay pervades our lives, denominates our worth, conditions our existence, and even defines our deaths. We are forever uncertain about what we are worth, and forever inquisitive about what the next man or woman is making. To satisfy such curiosity, this book offers an endless stream of puzzling, fascinating, surprising, and colorful figures. Few of us can resist looking up our own jobs to see if they fall within the going rate, the given salary parameters. It is a pastime as old as the economy and as current as tomorrow's classified page.

The first section of the book is a shameless exploitation of the economic voyeur that exists in all of us. The uncommon incomes of the not-so-private celebrities and notables in sports, politics, motion pictures, television, private industry, and so forth, are presented for relish or despair, for confirmation or outrage.

From the record, public and otherwise, pay scales, earnings data, surveys, research studies, and personal interviews, we examine how much people are earning for their daily bread and circuses. The result is a profile of personal income information, in general and specific, for America's working population.

The second section of the book consists of facts and figures pertaining to specific jobs—the nature of the work, the starting salary, the average salary, special pay or benefits. Within the ranks of 100 million American workers is a multitude of job categories. Since no selection could be considered comprehensive, we have tried to include those occupations that contain a wide variety of work situations. Subsequent editions may be more inclusive.

Sources of information are simply too extensive to cite, but we drew on government publications and surveys, information published by trade associations, unions, newspapers, magazines, books, and a plethora of data generated by private industry and the academic world.

We would like to take the opportunity to thank our editors, Carolyn Trager and Jo Goldberg, and the research writers who assisted us: Lois Cunniff, Meri Lobel, and Richard Siemanowski. Our thanks to Deirdre Evans Gittelman and Marcia Burick for their editorial concepts. Our thanks also to Meryl Marcus for secretarial assistance and Maurice B. Stiefel for his wise counsel. Naturally, we alone are responsible for errors of omission or commission.

$

PART ONE

Accounts Receivable

1

> Mind your till and till your mind.
> —C. H. SPURGEON

NET WORTH

PERSONAL ASSETS: CHEAP AT TWICE THE PRICE

One of the subtler by-products of inflation is the elevation of your true worth. In 1936 an average citizen weighing between 150 pounds and 160 pounds was valued at only $.98. By 1969, the chemical components of calcium, potassium, phosphate, magnesium, plus traces of other minerals, had risen in price, reaching $3.50. In the mid-seventies that figure rose to $5.60. By 1980, the market price of humans was $7.28. In contrast, for the purposes of cost-benefit analysis, the National Highway Traffic Safety Administration estimates that a human life, including the costs of medical attention and lost future earnings due to road accidents, is worth $287,175.

NET WORTH

In 1964, 3.3 million Americans were worth between $60,000 and $100,000. By 1972, 4.9 million Americans were worth that much. In that year, 9 percent of the population, approximately 12.8 million people, possessed over $60,000 in gross wealth. Of these, 10 percent had a net worth of $250,000 or more. These same 10 percent held nearly half the assets of those with over $60,000. At that time four out of ten households held liquid assets of under $500, and two out of ten had $5,000 or more. In 1980, the top 5.8 million households had an average net worth of $540,000. On the other side of the coin, 5.3 million families had virtually no savings and were existing below the official poverty level.

JUST YOUR AVERAGE MILLIONAIRE

The last time anyone looked, there were almost as many rich women as rich men. Among those with assets of $10 million or more, men average fifty-eight years of age, but women only forty. The average millionaire is usually over sixty. While a third of the affluent obtained their money through inheritance, most millionaires made it themselves.

Much less is known about the habits and behavior of the rich than about the poor, except for the occasional glimpses obtained from information released by the IRS. In recent years the IRS has started to compile an annual list of million-dollar returns. For example: in 1976 the number of taxpayers filing returns with incomes in excess of $1 million each was 1,149. By 1978 the number jumped to 2,000, an increase of 80 percent in two brief years.

While there are not all that many people earning a clear, taxable million dollars a year, the cumulative number of millionaires has grown, perhaps not exponentially but certainly at a double-digit rate. A study by the U.S. Trust Company estimates that 1 out of 426 citizens has assets of $1 million or more.

Millionaires are, of course, found all over the country, but the greatest density per state population is in Idaho, followed by Maine and North Dakota. The states with the highest numbers of wealthy people are: New York, California, Illinois, Ohio, Florida, New Jersey, Indiana, Idaho, Minnesota, and Texas.

Unfortunately, what inflation creates, inflation also takes away. A million bucks in 1940 bought a great deal more than it does today. In fact, a million 1940 dollars are worth only about $182,800 in goods and services now.

THE RICHEST OF THE RICH

When F. Scott Fitzgerald was writing in the twenties, there was probably some truth to his observation that the very rich "are different from you and me." There weren't many millionaires—and even fewer after the Great Crash. Today the differences have diminished, due to some redistribution of wealth. There are an estimated 520,000 millionaires in the United States. And being a millionaire certainly isn't what it used to be: indeed, it takes over $5.5 million today to achieve the same financial clout as $1 million did before World War II.

At one time, the richest man in the country, John Jacob Astor, could observe with tongue in cheek that "a man who has a million dollars is as well off as if he were rich." In some ways, a million dollars is no longer "serious" money. Perhaps one reason for this, inflation aside, stems from the mind-boggling number of ways of achieving wealth—many of them far from serious. For example, a fellow named Wally Amos did it by producing a superior chocolate chip cookie. Frank Perdue did it by selling chickens fed with, among other things, marigold petals in order to give them a yellow tinge—an image that obtains top chicken dollar. Berry Gordy founded Motown Industries, a record company specializing in soul and the Motown sound ("rats and roaches, love, guts and talent," says Gordy). Ray Kroc of McDonald's and R. David Thomas of Wendy's did it by selling hamburgers. Jeno Paulucci of ChunKing and Jeno's did it by using Italian spices in Chinese food and peddling frozen pizzas. Nolan Bushnell did it by developing video computer games in his company, Atari. Alan Silverstone did it by selling 1.5 billion gumballs annually from his U.S. Chewing Gum Manufacturing Company. The list goes on, from ballet dancers to basketball players, from authors of western novels to cat cartoonists—an endless, serendipitous journey, fueled by chutzpah and limited only by imagination.

Most people, including millionaires, regard the truly wealthy as a separate class from the recently rich rock singer, successful golf player, "in" artist, or silicon valley entrepreneur. With reverence they speak of the great fortunes: Rockefeller, Ford, Mellon, Du Pont. To be sure, these fortunes still exist, but usually in some fragmented form among third generation cousins, or institutionalized within the great foundations. Consequently, established wealth still exists but has less sanctified presence than before. Great fortunes today are relatively inconspicuous. Any list of richest individuals is likely to be conjecture, since private wealth need not be reported, except that portion which is derived from publicly owned companies. Consequently, any list is a guesstimate at best. Moreover, since so many fortunes are derived from listed shares on stock exchanges, the net value of holdings will fluctuate, sometimes drastically. The following list is not necessarily in order of magnitude; about the only thing you can say for certain is that these are indeed wealthy people.

Daniel K. Ludwig is probably the richest man in America, with personal wealth estimated to be over $3 billion. His fortune is derived from shipping. He is currently developing 500,000 acres in the Brazilian Amazon basin. The development, Jari, will either make another few billion for the Swiss cancer foundation, which Ludwig has bequeathed it to, or be one of the great fiascoes of all time. Henry Ford tried the same thing in the twenties, hoping to create a rubber plantation for his cars, but never succeeded.

Gordon P. Getty owns 38.7 percent of Getty Oil Company. While the price of the stock fluctuates, he is worth somewhere between $2.5 and $3.7 billion. Of course, it's the dividends that count—close to $64 million per year.

The Hunt brothers, and stepsisters, heirs to the fortune of daddy H. L. Hunt of Texas, may be cash poor after their silver shenanigans, but they are still silver rich. In their attempt to corner the market, they were nearly liquidated when the price fell from $50 an ounce to $10 an ounce and they were besieged with margin calls. They survived, but congressional hearings revealed that they own or control 93 million ounces of silver, worth $1.5 billion in a depressed market. In addition, the Hunts own 250 corporations in a diversity of fields, from sugar-beet refining and citrus groves to contract drilling and coal mining.

The Lykes family of Tampa and New Orleans, owners of another shipping-based conglomerate, has private holdings worth more than $1 billion.

Forrest E. Mars is head of what has been termed the nation's largest and most secretively held private company. His secret is candy bars. The Mars company, maker of such childhood favorites as Milky Ways, Mars Bars, and M&Ms, has created a billion-dollar fortune.

Paul Mellon is heir to the family banking house, plus aluminum and oil fortunes, created by his father, Andrew Mellon. He increased his net worth in the most felicitous fashion, by marrying the Warner Lambert Listerine heiress. His equity: $750 million. At one time the family was worth real money—in excess of $4 billion before bequests to children and foundations.

Leonard Stern is the son of the founder of Hartz Mountain Corporation, a pet food and supplies company. His father emigrated from Nazi Germany with the family fortune—2,000 canaries. The company was struggling along until Stern, a newly minted graduate from New York University, stepped in and offered shares of the company to the public in the sixties. Stern owned 70 percent of the corporation, a piece of the action worth over $700 million. After amassing all that public money, the company has now reverted to private status, probably amassing another fortune by buying up cheap shares. Among other assets, Stern owns a thousand acres of prime New Jersey land, reported to be worth at least $350 million.

Edwin C. Whitehead founded a medical electronics company, Technicon. When it went public Whitehead owned 90 percent of the company, a fact that made him for a short period an instant billionaire. The company, which was sold to Revlon, is now worth half that.

The Newhouse family, heirs of the late Samuel Newhouse, father of the newspaper and communication chain, owns no public corporation. In fact, Sam Newhouse had no office, but kept facts and files in his head. This private fief is thought to be worth $750 million.

Michel Fribourg, owner of Continental Grain, is a publicity-shy magnate who fled from his native Belgium at the outset of World War II. His personal worth is estimated to be half a billion dollars, and his privately held company (plus a hundred subsidiary companies) accounts for a quarter of international grain dealings.

Stephen D. Bechtel is also probably worth half a billion dollars. Bechtel Construction was inherited from his father, but the petrodollar pool of the Middle East has vastly enhanced company coffers since Bechtel is a prime contractor to the oil-exporting countries.

WHO OWNS WHAT

A Senate report published in the mid-1970s found that 122 of the country's largest corporations were effectively controlled by twenty-one large financial institutions such as banks, mutual funds, and insurance companies. These twenty-one financial institutions virtually controlled 41 percent of the voting rights of all common stock in the nation. The single most powerful entity was Morgan Guaranty Bank, the banker's bank, which was one of the five largest stockholders in fifty-six companies and the largest investor in twenty-seven companies.

In 1980, an updated Senate staff study found that the top levels of ownership in the leading one hundred American corporations are now controlled by as few as fifteen financial institutions, with Morgan still in the lead.

The next logical question to ask is: Who owns Morgan Guaranty Bank? It is owned by J. P. Morgan & Co., a publicly traded bank holding company. Its nearly thirty-nine million shares are owned by thousands of investors and 311 financial institutions.

PEOPLE'S CAPITALISM: A PORTRAIT

One out of six American adults own shares in publicly owned corporations. Ownership is split almost evenly between men and women, though women have a slight edge. The average household income of a shareowning family is more than $19,000, a doubling since the previous survey by the New York Stock Exchange in the mid-sixties. While more "capitalists" historically have lived in New York than in any other state, California took the lead in the sixties. The smallest number of shareholders live in North Dakota. The height of public participation in the nation's stock markets was in 1970, when thirty-one million Americans owned shares. The number dwindled to twenty-five million in 1975, but in 1980 the number had recovered to thirty million shareholders. The typical stockholder is forty-five and a half years old, with a portfolio worth $4,000. In 1975, the average stockholder was fifty-two and a half, with a portfolio of $10,000.

College graduates own more securities than any other group, and people with professional or technical occupations are more likely to be investors than any other category. However, there are more brokerage accounts from people with incomes between $15,000 and $25,000 than there are from individuals earning over $25,000. Though financial institutions hold 34 percent of the securities listed on the New York Stock Exchange, the majority of shares are still owned by individuals, even if that number is shrinking. The average public order on the New York Stock Exchange is $12,289, but only $5,576 in other equity markets. Nearly half of the public volume is bought on margin, that is, borrowed from a brokerage house.

BEST INVESTMENTS

The argument over what is the best investment is destined to remain unsettled, for it obviously depends on when one buys and when one sells. However, the abstract results for 1971–81 are in; they are informative but hardly predictive. According to Salomon Brothers, the investment banking house, the compound annual rate of return for major categories of holdings for the ten-year period ranks as follows:

1. Oil	30.8%
2. Gold	28
3. Oriental Carpets	27.3
4. U.S. Coins	27.1
5. U.S. Stamps	23.5
6. China, Ceramics	22.9
7. Silver	21.5
8. Rare Books	16.8
9. Old Masters	15.4
10. Farmland	14.6
11. Diamonds	14.5
12. Housing	10.3
13. Consumer Price Index	8.3
14. Stocks	5.8
15. Foreign Exchange	5.3
16. Bonds	3.8

Since gold entered the free market in 1975 it has been a spectacular performer, rising in 1980 to a peak of $875 per troy ounce, a gain of 2,000 percent, before falling to below $400 per ounce in 1981. Over the longer run, however, it performed less spectacularly, largely because its price was restricted by government intervention. From 1890 to 1975, the average return on both silver and gold was only 1 percent per year. In contrast, housing for the same period rose nearly 7 percent per annum.

COLLECTIBLE INVESTMENTS

Without a central auction market or interchangeable items, it is impossible to compare price appreciation among nonfinancial instruments. However, some recent records reveal that the inverted Curtiss Jenny airmail stamp, which was issued in 1918, soared to past $135,000—pound for pound undoubtedly the world's most expensive item. Meanwhile, the Gutenberg Bible has changed hands for $2 million.

DIAMONDS

Diamond prices soared in the late 1970s with the De Beers syndicate extracting a surcharge on its sales to wholesalers. Diamond jewelry—excluding engagement rings—is owned by 44 percent of American women over the age of fifteen. However, their investment potential may be more apparent than real. Example: Richard Burton bought his then wife Elizabeth Taylor a $1.2 million (solitaire) stone in 1969. A decade later it was sold at a handsome profit, for nearly $3 million—an average yearly yield of only 9.5 percent.

INTERNATIONAL PRICE LEVELS AND LIVING STANDARDS—1979

The following table compares the prices of a market basket consisting of more than 100 different consumer articles and services weighted by consumer habits. The table was prepared by the Union Bank of Switzerland with Zurich equaling 100 on the index.

City	
Jeddah	141
Abu Dhabi	125
Bahrain (Manama)	124
Tokyo	106
Oslo	104
Geneva	103
Copenhagen	102
Zurich	100
Düsseldorf	96
Buenos Aires	96
Tehran	95
Paris	95
Hong Kong	94
Brussels	89
Stockholm	89

City	
New York	84
Caracas	84
Luxembourg	83
Helsinki	81
Rio de Janeiro	81
London	81
Chicago	79
Amsterdam	79
Madrid	78
Vienna	78
Athens	78
San Francisco	77
São Paulo	75
Los Angeles	74
Tel Aviv	70
Singapore	70
Panama	70
Jakarta	69
Toronto	68
Sydney	68
Dublin	67
Montreal	67
Milan	65
Johannesburg	64
Bangkok	60
Bogotá	55
Mexico City	53
Istanbul	52
Lisbon	47
Manila	46

U.S. LIVING STANDARDS

Los Angeles is the most typical city in the country as far as the standard of living is concerned. According to a survey by Fabian Linden of the Conference Board, a business research organization, the standard of living (based on household incomes and living costs) is lowest in metropolitan Northeast cities and highest in urban centers of the South. Washington, D.C., has the nation's highest, due to an abundance of highly paid federal employees, and New York City the nation's lowest. Based on an index of 100, the living standards of eighteen major American cities are listed in ascending order:

New York	86.7
Boston	86.9
St. Louis	93.2
Philadelphia	94.2
Pittsburgh	98.6
Los Angeles	100.4
San Francisco	102.1
Minneapolis–St. Paul	103.0
Baltimore	106.9
Cleveland	107.1
Seattle	108.1
Chicago	110.8
Milwaukee	112.5
Atlanta	113.3
Houston	117.3
Detroit	118.2
Dallas	121.0
Washington, D.C.	128.8

In another survey, this one by the Bureau of Labor Statistics, the most expensive cities for a family of four to maintain a moderate standard of living in were Anchorage, Honolulu, Boston, and New York. To maintain that moderate living standard the family would need $29,682 in Anchorage; $28,488 in Honolulu; $27,029 in Boston; $26,749 in New York; and $25,203 in Washington. The bureau found that in the fall of 1980, on an average national level, a family would need $34,409 a year to maintain a higher standard of living, $23,134 for an intermediate standard, and $14,044 to maintain a lower living standard.

RICHEST PEOPLE IN THE WORLD

Abu Dhabi's citizens, sitting on their Arabian oil assets, have an average income of $70,000 for every man, woman, and child. The chief sheikh has a family income of $300 million annually.

SECRETS OF SWISS BANKS

According to the Swiss Central Bank, at the beginning of 1979, foreigners had on deposit more than $115 billion. Critics of the banks insist that the banks hold another $124 billion in securities and real estate for foreign interests.

AVERAGE SAVINGS PER PERSON: 1979

Switzerland	$8,280
Japan	5,628
Belgium	3,847
United States	3,780
Sweden	3,434
Denmark	2,957
Norway	2,874
France	2,868
Germany	2,831
Austria	2,787

GROSS NATIONAL PRODUCT PER PERSON: 1979

Kuwait	$17,270
Switzerland	14,240
Denmark	11,900
Sweden	11,900
West Germany	11,700
Belgium	10,890
United States	10,820
Norway	10,710
Netherlands	10,240
France	9,940
Canada	9,650
Japan	8,800
Australia	8,100
Austria	8,620
Saudi Arabia	7,370
United Kingdom	6,340
Italy	5,240
Israel	4,170
USSR	4,110
Venezuela	3,130
Korea	1,500
China	250
India	200
Ethiopia	100

2

What will become of virtue when
one must get rich at any price?
—RUSKIN

SHOW BIZ

PRESIDENTIAL PITCH

Ronald Reagan may be the first president to have endorsed commercial products—Chesterfield cigarettes, Van Heusen shirts, and General Electric goods—before arriving at the presidency. It is, of course, second nature for celebrities to tout products: from Lillie Langtry pitching Pears soap ("I have discarded all others") to Bill Cosby who first worked for Ford and then Chrysler: "Whatever money I made from Ford, I gave half of it to the government. The government, in turn, took my money and gave it back to Chrysler. I want to help Chrysler pay the government back." Frank Sinatra, Johnny Cash, Gregory Peck, and Sally Struthers are among the other big money-makers who tried to help Chrysler by promoting the "K" cars for a daily scale of $275.

Not all endorsements work as expected. Farrah Fawcett was paid $2 million to move her own line of hair products, without notable success. Roberto Duran's Seven-Up stint was dropped after he dropped out of his return match with Sugar Ray Leonard. Somehow the fizzle went out of his punch, or so thought the soda company. One cannot blame the celebrities for cashing in on their fame: fortune is fickle and one never knows when it will be either horse operas or the unemployment line. After all, Ronald Reagan was paid only $200 per week for his first flick.

ANOTHER OPENING—FOR VERY FEW

Theater performers, while they make nowhere near as much as their successful television or film colleagues, can still go home with a comfortable salary. The minimum wage for a Broadway show is $525 a week, and this number has been known to climb as high as $15,000 for really big stars.

The spots at the top, however, are few and far between. Of all the members of Screen Actors Guild, American Federation of Television and Radio Artists, and Actors Equity, about 3 percent make over $25,000 a year, and three-quarters make less than $2,500 a year. In 1980, the Screen Actors Guild and the American Federation of Television and Radio Artists negotiated a three-year agreement with a 32.5 percent increase in pay-scale minimums. Actors now receive a minimum of $298.12 per day, and $1,040.12 per week.

SINGING FOR YOUR SUPPER—PLUS

Billy Joel, the pop singing star, received $1.02 in royalties for every copy of his hit album *The Stranger* and $1.05 for another winner, *52nd Street. The Stranger* sold 7.4 million and *52nd Street* 6.4 million, which would make the royalties on those two albums amount to $14,268,000. That would be just enough not only to live on easy street but probably to buy it as well.

GOD BLESS AMERICA AND THE TUBE

In 1933, before the rise of that media giant, television, radio star Kate Smith was making $3,000 a week. The days of the great radio stars may be gone, but their modern-day counterparts, TV stars, can make, if they hit the top, incredible sums of money. Celebrity guests on the comedy "The Love Boat" make $5,000 for an appearance. Robin Williams makes $30,000 an episode for his role in "Mork and Mindy." Linda Gray and Victoria Principal of "Dallas" both make $10,000 an episode, while J.R., the villain, played by Larry Hagman, is paid $100,000 per show. Jaclyn Smith and Cheryl Ladd, of "Charlie's Angels," both make $50,000 a show.

The hotter the "property," of course, the more money

he/she can command (worth being gauged principally by the show's ratings). Carroll O'Connor, of the ever-popular "All in the Family," made $110,000 per episode.

WHATEVER HAPPENED TO THE CASTING COUCH?

Producers, of course, can sail or sink with any particular venture. As a result, their salaries can fluctuate greatly and be difficult to get a fix on. Some sources place the pay of a producer of a half-hour, prime-time sitcom at $7,000 to $10,000 a week. However, Bud Yorkin, cochairman of the Caucus for Television Producers, in discussing the cost of a television show versus what the networks will pay for it, has complained that "you can't live on a network fee." A feature film producer, taking a percentage of the gross, a fee, a salary, or all three, stands to make quite a bit if his film hits it big.

THIS IS HOWARD COSELL!

Howard Cosell, that most famous of sports journalists, makes more than $1 million a year. TV journalists who specialize, or those who do other than the broad, general news programs, often make more money as a result. For "60 Minutes," Mike Wallace makes about $500,000 a year. "Good Morning America" and "Today," two morning news-and-entertainment programs, are hosted by, respectively, David Hartman and Tom Brokaw. Tom Brokaw makes about $450,000, and Mr. Hartman makes $750,000 a year.

NO BIZ LIKE NEWS BIZ

Since the onset of the new "show biz" school of TV journalism, television journalists have become personalities as important, and sometimes as flashy, as any other television star, with anchorpeople, naturally, leading the procession of star-studded TV reporters. And, just as naturally, their salaries have risen accordingly.

Roger Grimsby, of ABC, the station that is generally acknowledged to have started it all, made an estimated salary of $250,000 a year in 1978. None of his major network rivals on the East or West Coast made less than $200,000. Of course, the real superstars of the business went well beyond that. Walter Cronkite, in 1979, did better than $700,000. When Barbara Walters was hired by ABC and given a $5 million, five-year contract, Harry Reasoner's pay was raised to $500,000 before he returned to CBS. The heir apparent of Walter Cronkite, whose own salary was in the neighborhood of three-quarters of a million per year, is Dan Rather, reportedly making $1.6 million annually.

MODEL MONEY

You don't always need curves to pander to male television viewers. Brooke Shields, the baby-faced teenage model and movie actress, earns as much as $10,000 a day to wear nothing between herself and her jeans. Her mother gives her $10 a week as an allowance.

THE GREATEST SHOW ON EARTH

Sixteen girls, count 'em—sixteen, are in each of the Ringling Brothers Barnum & Bailey Circus traveling units: the Red and the Blue. Each one travels different routes but with the exception of the head show girl in each unit they all get the same pay and share the same hazards.

For working thirteen to sixteen shows a week, doing four numbers each show, making it an eleven-to-fifteen-hour day, six days a week, the Ringling Brothers show girls get $225 per week. The head show girl gets an additional $15 per week.

The show girls are given stateroom accommodations on the circus train and are charged $10 for room and board. However, the stateroom is about 5 by 7 feet and is shared by two.

So much for the glamour of the circus—now how much is a ride on the back of an elephant down Broadway worth?

BE A CLOWN! BE A CLOWN! BE A CLOWN!

The underlying anguish of the operatic clown Pagliacci may have been the result of his concern for the financial state of his fellow American jesters.

Ringling Brothers Barnum & Bailey Circus has a three-year pay program for its apprentice clowns. The first year they receive $165 per week. The second year it's raised to $175 per week and if they make it to the third year—and many don't—they get another raise of $10 to $185 per week. After that it's whatever they can negotiate. But with the many aspiring clowns coming out of the circus "college" in Florida waiting in the wings, there isn't much leverage for negotiation. One benefit the clowns share with most of their circus colleagues is that $70 of their salary is considered living expenses and as a result is not taxable.

DON'T STEP IN THE *UNGOWA*

The unsung men of the circus world are the rootless, restless "working men" as they are called, who are responsible for the care, cleaning, and feeding of the horses and elephants. Now would it surprise you to know that they get—hold on now—$120 per week with the Ringling Brothers? What you certainly didn't know is that among their dubious "perks" is their right to buy "Dukie Books" for $35 worth of food that they can convert, in the old company-town tradition, in the circus "Pie Car" or dining car.

SOLO STARDOM

In the rarefied atmosphere of the megabuck, some individuals are industries unto themselves. Pelé, the soccer player, had a three-year contract with Warner Communications for $4.7 million. But this was eclipsed by Muhammad Ali's $8 million purse at age thirty-eight for a one-night boxing match, to recapture the title for the fourth time, up from $6 million he made in Manila in 1975. These latter salaries are due to the television rights, which means the fight is broadcast to a vast audience.

At this point sports figures compete with the superstars of the screen for compensation. The latest challenge is the $2 million movie. In recent years, Robert Redford was paid that for three or four weeks of work in *A Bridge Too Far*, and Marlon Brando also received a similar sum (plus 10 percent of the box-office gross) for his bit in *Apocalypse Now*. Not to be outdone is Jane Fonda, who received $2 million for *Her Brother's Keeper*. In point of history, however, the first $2 million was received by William Holden for *The Bridge on the River Kwai* back in the 1950s, but it was to be averaged out over a number of years. Some superstars are now nearing the $3 million mark, but there is no indication that the films are getting any better—only more expensive.

In the realm of entertainment, the highest paid performer is probably Johnny Carson, host of a late-night television talk show. Carson receives $5 million as the NBC master of ceremonies, plus more than a quarter of a million dollars per week for nightclub performances. His other sources of income, such as from endorsing clothes, earn him a total of between $12 and $15 million per year.

MOVIES OUT OF BOOKS

The connection between movies and books gets tighter all the time. A best-selling book is almost certain to have the movie rights bought—sometimes years before it is even considered for production. Sometimes the film rights are bought before the book is out, and sometimes the book is written after the movie.

Mario Puzo got $12,500 for the film rights to *The Godfather*. The film rights to his latest book, *Fools Die*, were sold for $1 million. According to sources, one film company commissioned, for $1 million, the writing of a novel, *Atlantic City*, with the specific intentions of making it a best-seller and then coming out with the film. And *Jaws 2*, by Hank Searle, a novelization of a sequel to a movie of a best-selling novel, sold close to four million copies and brought in about $840,000 in royalties.

THE CHICKEN CIRCUIT

Want to hear the inside scoop on the old Watergate scandal? The sum of $6,000 will get you G. Gordon Liddy, in the flesh, to tell about it. Want to reminisce about the fifties? An even $5,000 and Chubby Checker will do it for you. Recently, guest lecturing has become more popular than ever. Many celebrities have found it a quick and easy way to supplement their incomes. G. Gordon Liddy and his cohorts resorted to lecturing largely to help defray the costs of their huge legal fees resulting from the Watergate trial. And those on the way down from the top (or already at the bottom of the descent) use lecturing as a way to continue to capitalize on their onetime fame.

How about some tales of the post-Nixon White House? A mere $10,000 and Gerald Ford will be happy to entertain you and your friends with stories. The life of a veteran TV journalist? The same $10,000 will get Mike Wallace to act as raconteur for you. Want to know about the state of détente in the world today? Well, who better to hear it from than Henry Kissinger himself, a steal at $15,000 a shot. Yes, it seems that everyone has a tale to tell, if the price is right.

FAR FROM BUSTED

To some movie fans, seeing their favorite star peddling products on television is a bit of a comedown, and for that reason many names in the business will not "sell out." Cary Grant has refused all inducements for years. Sir Laurence Olivier, the epitome of class, was finally lured into selling Polaroid cameras. Of course, touting products is highly profitable, and as Bob Hope remarked, "You don't even have to take your clothes off." Consequently, stars can develop champagne tastes for selling beer. James Coburn endorsed Schlitz Light Beer in six commercials for $500,000—or about 208,000 six-packs at the going rate. And the $450,000 the late John Wayne received for Datril must have taken care of a lot of financial headaches. In some cases, the tie-ins are a natural. Jane Russell's rise to stardom was propelled by Howard Hughes and a push-up bra he designed for her to wear in the movie *The Outlaw*. Her television commercials promoting a line of brassieres for ample bosoms bring her about $110,000 per year.

3

> Take all your savings and buy some good stock and hold it till it goes up and then sell it. If it don't go up, don't buy it.
>
> —WILL ROGERS

BIZ BIZ

GREAT FORTUNES

Certainly the premier American corporations pay their heads exceedingly well; at least two dozen draw salaries and bonuses that exceed $1 million annually. If options and stock rights are set aside, only seven chief executive officers receive $1 million or more in salary and bonuses. However, great fortunes are made both by running significant corporations and by owning a piece of them. Consequently, chief executives have increasingly insisted upon stock options or stock appreciation rights to compensate for their entrepreneurial efforts. The industries that pay their top operating people the most are aerospace, entertainment, and energy; the surge of oil prices has pushed petroleum executives into astronomic income levels if their compensation is in any way tied to profits or sales. There are twenty-five executives with compensation packages in excess of $1 million, though ironically only one had a straight salary in excess of that magic figure—Lee A. Iacocca. Because of Chrysler's troubles he skipped his salary altogether, though he did take the compensation promised when he left Ford.

A survey by the Conference Board revealed that roughly half of the chief executives of major corporations have a net worth in excess of $1 million, and that 10 percent of them have a net worth of over $5 million.

As might be expected, the highest paid executive in the United States comes from that make-believe world of Hollywood—indeed the entertainment business accounts for five out of the top thirteen.

In 1980, a stellar year for oil company earnings thanks to OPEC's oil shock, of the top two dozen executives half are from energy or oil equipment companies. According to *Business Week*'s annual survey, the highest compensated company official was Robert A. Charpie, president of Cabot Corporation, whose total package came to $3.3 million. However, he didn't do quite as well as Frank E. Rosenfelt, head of Metro-Goldwyn-Mayer Film Co., who earned (with stock options and incentives) a record $5.1 million the previous year.

TOP EXECUTIVE PAY

The *average* salary for the top people of America's major companies is $351,900. Of companies that gross less than $500 million, the median salary is $186,000 and for companies with revenues of $5 billion or more the average is $542,000.

Needless to say, almost all CEOs of major corporations are white men. While company hopping is an accepted way for middle management to become senior management (indeed one out of three middle managers has a job résumé in circulation), the top CEOs have been with their companies an average of twenty-five years and have been the operating boss for eleven years. Apparently, there is more stability in the senior ranks of corporate life than is reflected in the financial press. Finally, the average age for major CEOs is fifty-eight.

BOARD OF DIRECTORS

Outside members of corporate boards do reasonably well for their monthly meetings: manufacturing companies pay their outside directors a median fee of $11,500 per year, while financial companies pay their outside members $8,000. As might be predicted, large corporations pay their directors considerably more, an average of $20,400. Considering the fact that outside directors spend an average of 105 hours on company business, the typical rate is $110 an hour.

"PERKS" AT THE TOP

For the highest paid executives of the Fortune 1000 the chief perquisite is the corporate automobile, followed by life insurance, club membership, liability and travel insurance. As a percentage of total pay, the average "perk" value ran between 1 and 11 percent, with 3 to 4 percent being the average for the most senior executives. For 70 percent of all executives in major corporations, the average value was under $5,000, but for the very top 5 percent they were worth over $25,000.

HIGHEST PAID WOMAN EXECUTIVE

While there are a few women who make more money as partners or owners of businesses, such as Mary Wells Lawrence, chairman and chief executive officer of an advertising agency, Wells, Rich, Greene Inc., probably the highest paid female was Jane Cahill Pfeiffer, chairman of the National Broadcasting Company. Her salary was $225,000 per year plus an annual bonus of at least $200,000 before she was fired by then president Fred Silverman. (If her ego was bruised, she at least took comfort in the settlement to buy out her contract—for a mere $500,000. Still, she didn't do quite as well as John D. Backe, president of CBS, when he departed that network with a $2 million settlement.) Katharine Graham, owner of the *Washington Post* and other communications companies, earns a salary of $375,000. But then, she inherited the shop. Inheritances are, of course, nice, but a growing number of women have made it without that initial advantage. Probably the highest paid woman consultant is a onetime Miss America, Bess Myerson, now a professional consumer advocate. Banks and soap companies paid her $493,000 in consulting fees the year she ran unsuccessfully for a U.S. Senate seat.

Heidrick and Struggles, an executive search firm, looked at women officers in thirteen hundred large business organizations. They found that women tended to occupy posts such as assistant secretary (40 percent) and group vice president, senior vice president, or vice president (24 percent). Only 0.8 percent of the sampling were chairmen, vice chairmen, or presidents. Most corporate openings were in the East (40 percent) followed by the Midwest (29 percent), and most positions fell into the fifty-plus age group (41 percent). Most women (29 percent) earned between $20,000 and $29,000, while 18 percent of the women responding to the study earned $60,000 or more. Overall, the latest figures suggest that there are 288,000 women in the labor force earning at least $25,000 a year. The search firm could find only 497 women officers in the thirteen hundred corporations. Of that group, 8.6 percent earned $100,000 a year or more. Most of the women officers (60 percent) earned less than $50,000 per year, compared to male counterparts who averaged $134,500.

UNION SCALE

If a million-dollar payoff is the goal of top corporate brass, the $100,000 payday is the more modest aim of top union brass. Since stock options and bonuses are usually out of the question, about the only perk is the union car, and in some instances a house. Allowances and expenses substantially increase the total compensation package.

Twenty-one union leaders had 1980 pay packets worth more than $100,000. The highest paid was the late Frank E. Fitzsimmons, who took home $174,794. His successor, Roy L. Williams, was given a raise to $225,000. Some other union leaders received even more money, but that was a result of double or triple compensation from holding multiple offices.

4

Poverty is no disgrace to a man,
but it is confoundedly inconvenient.
—REV. SIDNEY SMITH

THE ARTS

FAME AND FORTUNE

At one time, entrance into the arts was a guarantee of perpetual poverty. History is replete with penniless composers, penurious writers, and profligate painters. The notion of a carefree *la vie Bohème* was a fiction of romanticism lauding life-style over lucre. Dr. Johnson, of course, had it right when he said that "no man but a blockhead ever wrote except for money."

Artists are still working for fame and fortune, though in today's media world the accent increasingly is on the latter. Within the last generation promoted work has racked up unheard of sums. Harold Robbins, the novelist, earns $35,000 per working day from his writings, Neil Simon received an advance of $750,000 for a couple of paragraphs outlining *The Odd Couple*, and Alex Haley made $5 million from *Roots*. In the previous century Edgar Allan Poe, the father of the mystery story, rarely saw more than a couple of hundred dollars for a story and received $10 for his poem "The Raven." Mark Twain wrote for seven cents a word, which is why, he once remarked, "I never write 'metropolis' because I get the same price for 'city.' " The difference between nineteenth- and twentieth-century pay scales and remuneration is naturally startling; however, the present spread between the superstars and toilers in the vineyards is almost as great. Baryshnikov, the émigré ballet dancer, performed with the American Ballet at $200,000 a year until he left for the New York City Ballet Company, where his pay dropped to $150,000. In the corps de ballet, the average union dancer earns about $12,000 a year, with the American Guild of Musical Artists insisting on a minimum of $227 a week.

MAESTRO PLEASE

Instrumentalists and vocalists are rather late to the dinner table—the great maestros preceded them. Toscanini started with NBC's symphony orchestra in the thirties at $4,000 per broadcast, plus the modest perk in those days of the network picking up his income tax bill.

In the seventies, the *Times* of London cited Sir Georg Solti, Leonard Bernstein, Herbert von Karajan, Karl Böhm, and Carlo Maria Giulini as the top five earners, putting away an average of $162,000 for a couple of dozen concerts with their regular orchestras. Today, Bernstein and Solti command $15,000 per concert. In addition, royalty income allows Sir Georg to gross nearly a million dollars annually.

MUSIC TO THEIR EARS

Today, a solo instrumentalist of the first rank, an Isaac Stern or a Vladimir Horowitz, can command close to $10,000 to $40,000 a concert, and sometimes a percentage of the box-office revenue. Back in 1872 pianist Anton Rubinstein toured America for $200 per concert.

Jean Pierre Rampal earns $250,000 a year and plays only on a gold flute, of which he has several, and James Galway makes a similarly comfortable living on his two gold, two silver, and two of a golden alloy—one with a diamond on the end of it. However, not many other flautists make much more than the minimum wage.

Though Joan Sutherland and Luciano Pavarotti can command $25,000 to $40,000 per concert, there are only twenty opera singers who can make a living from professional singing.

ART AS AN INVESTMENT

Objets d'art are widely touted as sound investments and inflation hedges. Are they? The British research organization, the

Economist Intelligence Unit, looked at prices for 182 art works in fourteen categories that were sold at auction at least twice between 1960 and 1980. The auction prices were then matched to both the Financial Times index of London Stock Exchange industrials and the Dow Jones industrial index (with dividends reinvested).

Of the 182 art works, 69 percent outperformed the indexes, and 3 percent were equal to them. However, the remaining 28 percent brought prices that were less than the equities indexes.

Some of the categories of art that did extraordinarily well were modern paintings, modern prints, and books—all consistently showing 100 percent gains over market indexes. Some of the worst performers were Chinese jade, American paintings, Impressionist paintings, and English drinking glasses.

The best performers did very well indeed, both in relation to the percentage increase of the second sale over the first, and also compared to the equities indexes. For example: René Magritte's painting *Un Simple Histoire d'Amour* in two decades rose 4,651 percent, from $1,111 to $52,800. An Old Testament in Greek rose 3,448 percent, from $1,364 to $48,400, a Ming stem cup was up 2,558 percent, from $5,720 to $153,780, and a modern print by Edvard Munch, *Evening on the Beach,* rose 2,314 percent, from $3,097 to $74,800.

The worst performers improved in price, for the most part, but did poorly compared to the stock averages. A Dutch delft tureen of 1765 increased by 14 percent, from $23,100 to $26,400, but was down by 208 percent compared to stocks. A Gilbert Stuart of Ozias Humpred fell in price by 28 percent, from $19,800 to $14,300, and declined by 168 percent compared to the averages.

While the study allowed for buying and selling expenses in both art and equities, there is a substantial hidden cost in maintaining a rare object—insurance, storage, and air conditioning. Nevertheless, investment in quality art certainly has been worthwhile.

THE ARTIST'S LIFE

In general, collecting art has been much more lucrative thar creating it. Traditionally, works of great masters and posthumous art of just about any age had value due to aesthetic taste and finite quantities.

For example, in the New York art market no fewer than eleven paintings fetched $1 million at auctions in 1980. The staggering auction was that of a Turner, *Juliet and Her Nurse*, which set a world record of $6.4 million (plus a 10 percent buyer's fee), surpassing the last record sale of Velásquez's *Portrait of Juan de Pareja* for $5.5 million. The painting was sold by Flora Whitney Miller, the daughter of Gertrude Vanderbilt Whitney who founded the Whitney Museum. Experts had expected that the painting would receive no more than $2 million in bids since it is not regarded as one of Turner's finest works.

Living artists have rarely sold well, but that changed in the sixties as the works of Abstract Expressionists commanded great sums. Picasso was obviously an example of an extraordinary living talent in the megabuck range, breaking the old rule that the only rich artist was a dead one. The art work of Jackson Pollock, Mark Rothko, and Alexander Calder created multi-million-dollar estates, but their works sold for substantial prices even before they died. Andrew Wyeth is probably the highest paid American artist, with quarter-million-dollar paintings. The Department of Labor and the National Endowment for the Arts find that the number of artists and sculptors rose from 130,000 in 1970 to 193,000 in 1980. The vast majority are unable to make 1 percent of what Wyeth receives.

THE BRUSH OFF

Artists do not benefit from secondary sales or auctions of their works (though there is a movement to pay them royalties and a law to that effect in California), but certainly such sales establish a floor for prices of present and future works. The relatively recent upsurge in the price of works by living artists has more to do with the value of money than the worth of art. Sam Salz, a New York art dealer, notes that "pictures didn't become expensive, money became cheap. It's not the pictures that aren't worth the money, it's the money that isn't worth the money anymore."

This last statement is an epitaph for our times as inflation distorts the true worth of everything—especially one's labors. The danger is not that we will know the price of everything, but the value of nothing.

THE BOOK BUSINESS

It is estimated that about forty thousand titles are published yearly, a total of 1.64 billion books in hard and soft cover. It is also estimated by trade sources that almost two-thirds of them lose money. Nevertheless, the publishing industry sells at retail $7.2 billion worth of books. Most of the money is made by the sale of reference works and textbooks, but the megabuck deals are generated in the trade departments. As a rule, royalty payments to trade authors range between 10 and 15 percent of a hardcover book's list price; on paperbacks the royalty is usually split fifty-fifty by author and hardcover publisher.

Since royalties are cumulative over the years, it is difficult to know how much a book finally earns. But the hyperbolic advances—matched sometimes only by book jacket blurbs—are public record. James Michener reportedly earned $2 million in royalties from the sale of one million copies of his novel *Chesapeake*. In the sale of book club rights to his *The Covenant*, he picked up $1.75 million. Other recent blockbusting advances have been paid for paperback rights to Judith Krantz for *Princess Daisy*, $3.2 million; to Robin Cook for a joint package of *Sphinx* and *Brain*, $3 million; to Mario Puzo for *Fools Die*, $2.55 million; to Phil Donahue for his autobiography, $1.63 million; to Avery Corman for his *The Old Neighborhood*, $1.45 million.

Not all authors are so fortunate. A Columbia University survey of American authors found that the average author earns less than $5,000 per year. The top 10 percent, however, do better and earn $45,000 per year, while the top 5 percent have incomes of $80,000 or above.

5

Money is like manure—
good only when spread around.
—SANDBURG

THE SPORTING LIFE

SWINGING FOR THE FENCES

Escalating salaries in the sports world not only outpace inflation, but even tax the imagination since the pay is for play, not work. For instance, the average big league baseball player was catching $22,000 a year in 1970 to take home. That figure was about twice the median family income. By 1980, the average earnings for a major leaguer were $143,756, seven times the earnings of the average family. At the apex of his career Babe Ruth was earning $100,000 a year—but then it was worth at least five times more than it is today.

FREE AGENTS AND FREE TRANSPORTATION

In the mid-seventies baseball players left the world of indentured servitude and became free to negotiate their own pay scales. Since ball players have a relatively short professional life—an average of less than five years—it was understandable that they wished pay packages substantial enough to protect them against the revenue agent and the ravages of time. Along with corporate executives, a few baseball players are now seeing million-dollar paydays. Nolan Ryan of the Houston Astros has a four-year contract for $4 million, once something of a record-breaker. Such luminaries as Dave Parker, Pete Rose, and Rod Carew are now earning $800,000 to play the summer game. Phil Niekro, a knuckleball pitcher for the Braves, has not only a $3 million deal that promises to keep him in rice and beans until the contract expires in December 2010, but also a clause guaranteeing a new Cadillac Seville each year for the next three years.

YANKEE CLIPPER

The newest entrant into the million-dollar club is Dave Winfield, an outfielder for the Yankees, who signed on for ten years for $25 million. Whether he will be worth more than Reggie Jackson, who signed a contract for $2.66 million for five years, only time will tell. Winfield's base salary is $1.5 million per year for ten years. In addition, he received $1 million for signing, a cost-of-living allowance of $3 million, which is compounded annually, plus incentive money of $1 million for winning the Most Valuable Player award and other awards.

MARATHON MAN ON THE RUN

Winning eight marathon runs in Boston and New York, Bill Rodgers has made a profitable career in what was essentially an amateur sport before the sponsors and promoters got to it. He has run a long way since 1976, when he earned $10,000 as a teacher. From seminars, endorsements, clinics, sales conferences, and his own shops he makes between $200,000 and $250,000 a year. On the other side of the balance sheet, Rodgers must run 120 miles a week to keep in shape.

TAKE ME OUT TO THE BALL GAME

As you walk through the gates of a stadium to see a baseball game, you will notice the attendant taking your ticket; he will make $35.00 for that game. The usher who brings you to your seat will make $18.50 (before tips, of course). When you raise your voice with the rest of the fans because the umpire called your man out, it might interest you to know that he is making $22,000 a year for his opinions, unless he is a veteran of over twenty years, in which case it would be $50,000. And of all those players on the field, not one man is making less than $21,000 a year.

BABY, YOU'VE COME A LONG WAY

Companies have been sponsoring sports on radio and television for a very long time. Who can forget when the Friday night fights were brought to you by Blue Blades and the sign in center field touted the Breakfast of Champions? In the last few years, however, corporations have moved away from buying commercial advertising time and space. Instead they are creating sporting events. Anheuser-Busch spends $20 million a year backing everything from a hydroplane racer and Miss Budweiser to six rodeo riders (obviously called "The Six Pack") and even Paul Newman's Can-Am racing team.

And along with the creation of these tourneys, trials, cups, championships, and series goes the prize money. Jack Kramer, the tennis pro, was the first to organize the Grand Prix tennis circuit. Today there are ninety-two events around the world in which male tennis players compete, offering over $14 million in prize money. In recent years top player Bjorn Borg has earned more than $2 million a year, much of it from awards, but some of it from being a walking billboard. For wearing a headband for a home brew he earned $50,000—no sweat. Women's tournaments are only slightly less rich, with prize money totaling about $9 million. Chris Evert Lloyd appears to be the leading lady for superbucks, but Tracy Austin and Martina Navratilova are up-and-coming contenders.

BIG MONEY, SMALL MONEY

Hardly a day goes by without headlines of another record-breaking contract for some star jock. The net effect has been to raise salaries throughout the sports world and bring team salaries up to unheard of levels in 1981. Baseball players now have average salaries of $170,000 per season; basketball players $167,000; hockey players $100,000; and football players $60,000.

On the other side of the coin, batboys average between $15 and $20 per game; ball boys or girls in tennis run for the minimum wage, $3.20 per hour; and even the Dallas Cowgirls cheer for $15 per day.

BET MY MONEY ON THE BOBTAIL NAG

In the mid-seventies over ninety million Americans were betting some $22 billion a year. Even though chances of winning in horse racing are considered worse than in any other form of gambling, horse racing was the favorite pastime. Recently, casino gambling has begun closing the gap.

The Institute for Social Research of the University of Michigan has found the following characteristics among gamblers: there are more men than women; the very young (eighteen to twenty-four) gamble more than any other age group; there are an equal number of employed and unemployed; divorced people bet more than married; college graduates gamble more than high school graduates and twice as much as people who didn't finish high school; Catholics bet more than Jews who bet more than Protestants; atheists bet far less than people with religious beliefs; the Northeast bets twice as much as the South.

Finally, of the adults who gamble, the average annual legal outlay is roughly $400.

IT'S NO BULL

If there is any profession that has an aura of romance that masks the toughness and meager wages one can expect, it is that of the cowboy. And these days the only place they can look for any real money is the rodeo. The most treacherous ride the cowboy can take is on the back of a bull—where the danger is long and the prize money is short.

Don Jay at twenty-six has been the world champion bull rider five times and while on the top made $60,000 in prize money at the price of almost countless stitches and bone bruises. As for the rest of the five thousand members of the Rodeo Cowboys Association, if they made expenses and entry fees, they were lucky.

The richest prize in rodeo history—$18,500—was awarded for each of the following events: bull riding, calf roping, saddle bronc riding, and barrel racing. A woman, Carol Goostree, won the barrel racing in 33.19 seconds.

6

God gave me my money.
—J. D. Rockefeller

IT'S BETTER TO RECEIVE

CHARITY

Every day private Americans, corporations, and their non-governmental institutions give $100 million to assorted charities, from the ASPCA to the Zoological Society, not to mention charities with such purposes as planting trees in the Holy Land, exploring interplanetary space, and instructing monkeys in modern art. The $40 billion charity industry is a tax-free expression of a generous people—donating $180 per citizen every year. Thirty-nine percent of the corporate largesse went to health and welfare causes, while 60 percent of private moneys went to religious causes. The most generous corporations, the ones with the most to give, were those in the petroleum business. Corporations prefer to give to other institutions. Their support of the arts is a case in point: the Business Committee for the Arts Incorporated has estimated that in 1979 business gave $436 million to the arts. The largest recipients were museums, which received $0.19 of each donated dollar; individual artists received less than $0.005 of each corporate contribution.

FOUNDATION GIVING AND GETTING

There are those in this country who make a living of our giving, that is, dispensing funds in the form of grants through various foundations. After all, when a group like the Ford Foundation has assets well in excess of $2.7 billion, a competent executive staff is quite necessary to handle the comings and goings of all that money. And some of these corporate Kriss Kringles take in pretty enviable salaries themselves. Franklin Thomas, president of the Ford Foundation, has a salary of about $135,000, plus employee benefits of over $30,000. The president of the Rockefeller Foundation earns a similar salary for giving away $42 million.

GIVING IT AWAY

"They don't give like they used to" is a cry heard on every skid row around the world. John D. Rockefeller gave away $750 million pre-1938 dollars (roughly equivalent to $4.5 billion). His grandson John D. Rockefeller III left a paltry $94 million to charity.

RURAL POVERTY

Of all "officially" poor people in the United States, 39 percent live in rural areas—which according to the Census Bureau contain less than one-third of our population. Furthermore, roughly half of the nation's poor still live in the South, the rise of the Sun Belt notwithstanding.

WHO'S POOR

Every year the government estimates those who fall into the category of "non-resource persons." Poverty is determined by food expenses that are presumed to take up a third of a family budget. Using an economy food plan as a base figure, the government multiplies by three to find the basic poverty line.

In 1981, a nonfarm family of four was considered poor if its income was below $8,450. A single person was poor if his income was below $4,310. For a family of six, the line was drawn at $11,210.

Before World War I, three-fifths (60 percent) of the nation's citizenry were living at or below the poverty line. After World War II, the figure had decreased to 33 percent.

In 1959, before the social welfare programs of the 1960s, 22 percent of the American population was considered poor. By 1969 the poor made up only 12 percent of the population, a figure that has remained fairly stable through the 1970s.

The poverty level is calculated without regard to transfer payments, rent supplements, food stamps, Medicaid, Medicare, and other in-kind payments. If these were included perhaps only 3 percent of the population would be classified as poor, according to Morton Paglin, a professor of economics at Portland State University.

ESTATE TIME

Mae West died at age eighty-seven, leaving $1 million in real estate to her sister. By entertainment standards she died with only modest holdings. By contrast, John Lennon's estate at the time of his death was estimated to be on the order of $235 million, with recording royalties pouring in daily. Jack Benny, the penny-pinching comedian, left an estate valued at $4 million, plus instructions for the daily delivery of one rose to his wife, Mary Livingston.

7

A man can have more money
than brains, but not for long.
—ANONYMOUS

READING, RITING, AND RICHES

DEGREES STILL COUNT

Status aside, educational degrees are golden steppingstones. Christopher Jencks, a sociologist, says that his surveys indicate a student completing high school will earn 15 to 20 percent more than one who didn't. Completion of studies at a four-year college will account for a 49 percent earnings advantage over those with just high school diplomas. Moreover, by attending a "selective" college rather than a "nonselective" one, a student will earn more during his/her working career.

VOCATIONAL TRAINING

At the post-high-school level, 4 percent of the population is receiving or has recently completed vocational training. Contrary to popular belief, family income of students shows no relationship to the composition of the student body: they come in equal proportions from all economic levels.

BUSINESS SCHOOLS

President Calvin Coolidge in 1925 remarked that the "business of America is business"; 535 colleges in the United States have taken his word as gospel and established graduate-level business schools. With a Master of Business Administration (M.B.A.), a graduate can look forward to earning almost 100 percent more than a graduate from a liberal arts school. Indeed, graduates of the premier business schools such as Harvard, Stanford, Wharton, Chicago, and Columbia presently receive a median starting salary of $28,000. The average starting salary for all new M.B.A.'s in 1980 was $22,900.

Naturally, M.B.A.'s go into the business world: a plurality of graduates from Harvard and Michigan took jobs in manufacturing. At New York University the largest number of graduates went into commercial banking, followed by accounting, food processing, consulting and research, and energy. M.B.A.'s do less well than new lawyers by a couple of thousand dollars, but $10,000 to $15,000 better than teachers leaving graduate schools.

WHERE THE YOUTH ARE

A look at American youth by the Carnegie Commission, in 1980, finds that in the sixteen-to-twenty-one age bracket, most are already employed (41 percent). As for the rest, 38 percent are in high school or college, 6 percent are unemployed, 6 percent are homemakers, 5 percent are unoccupied (not looking for work), 3 percent are in the armed forces, and 1 percent are in institutions.

A MATTER OF DEGREE

A survey of high-level executives by the management school of UCLA and the personnel agency Korn/Ferry International finds that 43 percent have graduate degrees. Of the executives with advanced sheepskins, 41 percent have M.B.A.'s, 26 percent have law degrees. Fully a fifth received their graduate honors from Harvard.

STUDENT INCOME

Uncle Sam provides 972,000 college students with grants and loans totaling nearly $1.2 billion, with an average per student of $1,230.

WOMEN'S SMARTS

One of the outgrowths of the women's rights movement is the marked change in women's career goals and expectations. From 1966 through 1978, the number of women college students majoring in business multiplied fourfold. Indeed, women joined men to make the study of business the most popular major at the college level. The reverse side of this action was the steady decrease of women from their traditional fields of education and liberal arts.

Blacks showed the same pattern in their educational choices. Not only did black attendance at college triple, but their fields of study underwent major restructuring. In the sixties 40 percent majored in education or social sciences. By the end of the seventies, this figure dropped to 17 percent. Business is now the leading subject—having increased fivefold in popularity.

RAISING JUNIOR

Raising children is an expensive sport, more so than most families think. Thomas J. Espenshade of the Urban Institute has added it all up and come up with the staggering figure of $85,000 for basic maintenance from birth through four years of public college. These are out-of-pocket expenses per child, without allowing for additional earnings that the mother lost by staying home. Depending on her skills and ability, she might have earned between $15,000 and $55,000, or more. Housing, at $24,711, is the single largest expense in child rearing. However, if the family opts for a well-known private college, the $9,784 for four years of public college costs must be multiplied by a factor of four. Harvard and Yale now charge over $10,000 for tuition, room, and board.

In the 1930s a child could be raised for $7,766—about three times a family's annual earnings.

On the other hand, the College Placement Council reports that today's typical college graduate with a bachelor's degree in the humanities starts work at $12,888; in accounting at $16,956; in computer sciences at $18,696; and in petroleum engineering to $26,244.

FACULTY INCOME

The average base salary for faculty incomes in institutions of higher learning is $22,170 per year. Since it is hardly a king's ransom, college teachers are prominent members of the subterranean economy. Indeed, one survey found that nearly half of all faculty members earned outside income to supplement their pay. On average, they managed to increase their earnings by 22 percent, that is, $4,811. Full professors made the fullest use of their talents: 94 percent had outside income, averaging $8,914.

8

It would be thought a hard government
that should tax its people
one-tenth of their time,
to be employed in its service.
—BENJAMIN FRANKLIN

PUBLIC SERVANTS

POLITICAL PAYOFFS

Perhaps the oldest rule in politics is that politicians will take whatever they can get away with. Presumably, the president of the United States should be worth more than the president of General Motors, but $200,000 is the salary for running the country (plus $50,000 of tax-free expenses) compared with a $942,000 salary (and bonus) for making motor vehicles in the last good year the company had in 1979. And the mayor of the largest city in the country, New York, should be worth more than the CEO of Ford, but the former is paid only $60,000, while the latter is paid over $600,000. There might be a moral here if the private sector was outperforming the public one, but that hardly seems the case. It has taken as long to give the country an energy policy as it has an energy-efficient car. However, the real reason for the enormous difference has less to do with performance and more to do with a perception of what the public will allow civil servants. Of course, profit-making organizations are prone to rewarding successful capitalists—men and women who increase a corporation's profits by taking risks. Observers of the managerial scene suspect that many executives climb to the top of the greasy pole by not taking too many risks. Be that as it may, the public is bemused by pay differentials, occasionally upset but seemingly unmoved to adjust the inequalities.

Americans are not ungenerous to their political leaders, but cannot compare to the roughly $3 million a year the English support Queen Elizabeth II and the royal household with. The French pay their president, François Mitterrand, the equivalent of $80,000 a year. Chief executive officers in some Third World countries have very modest incomes, as do Eastern bloc leaders, but perks are often the socialist equivalents of high salaries. Perhaps the most austere regime is that of the Iranian Ayatollah Khomeini, who reportedly lives on a mere $30 per day. The contrast with his predecessor, of course, is overwhelming. Mohammed Riza Pahlevi, who possessed one of the largest private fortunes in the world, was reported by bankers to be worth at least $2 billion, and perhaps as much as $4 billion at the end of his reign. Nevertheless, the Iranian annual budget for the "Supreme leadership of State" allocated $43 million a year for the Shah's day-to-day living expenses—a per diem of $117,808.

Leading government figures are certainly not starving, but the level of their remuneration requires a monetary sacrifice if they are coming from the private sector. On the other hand, they are also paid in psychic income—prestige, fame, glory, power, and, of course, future connections to lubricate their postgovernmental period. Most recent American presidents were millionaires when they came to that high office, and for those that weren't, such as Eisenhower and Ford, sale of their memoirs banished any intimations of poverty.

Former President Carter arrived at the presidency with a net worth of roughly $1 million: it started humbly enough in his fertilizer business when he would gross a profit of $3 a ton for distributing the product. Ronald Reagan did very well in movies, but before becoming the Republican candidate he was making nearly $300,000 per year from his own form of political speaking engagements. Earning fees ranging from $2,500 to $10,000 per occasion, he not only charged the GOP for fund-raising events, but even the Boy Scouts of America. His two-year effort was valuable enough to push his net worth over the $4 million mark.

As chief central banker, the chairman of the Federal Reserve Board, Paul Volcker, had to take a cut in salary when he moved from the New York Federal Reserve Bank: the former pays only $60,000 compared with $110,000 a year for the latter. In 1980,

BankAmerica paid its then chief executive, A. W. Clausen, $709,085 and Chase's David Rockefeller received $618,000 before stock options and other perks. Another example of the poverty of public institutions: the prestigious secretary general of the United Nations, Kurt Waldheim, receives a base salary of $106,500 yearly, but his perks include a private housekeeping staff and luxury accommodations when he travels with his retinue. Curiously, the new president of the World Bank, A. W. Clausen, earns more in this United Nations agency than the secretary general. For distributing the billions, with equanimity if not equitability, he receives $115,000 a year.

PRESIDENTIAL SALARIES THEN AND NOW

Ronald Reagan and Jimmy Carter, the two latest holders of the office of chief executive, both commanded a figure of $200,000 as president of the United States plus a $50,000 expense budget. Taking into account the effects of inflation, while earlier presidents earned lower salaries, they actually made almost as much, or more in terms of buying power.

In 1949, Harry S. Truman had a yearly salary of $100,000, which would be worth $300,000 today. George Washington, local Virginia boy who made good, had a salary of $25,000 and back then in 1789, that amount would buy what is worth about $100,000 today. President Ulysses Grant made $50,000 a year; today that would be worth about $400,000. William H. Taft's salary of $75,000 has a contemporary equivalent of more than $500,000. And as recently as 1969, when Richard Nixon was making the same as President Reagan does today, that salary was worth twice what it is now.

WHAT THE HOUSE HOLDS

Congressional financial holdings are generally conservative: almost two-thirds of congressmen's funds are in real estate; nearly two-fifths hold mutual funds, stocks, and bonds; almost a third hold their funds in banks. Seventeen members have assets in excess of $1 million, almost equally divided between Republicans and Democrats. Contrary to popular opinion, outside honorariums averaged only $10,000, before the statutory limit of $8,625 came into effect in 1979, compared with the annual salary of $60,663. House members, on the average, hold investments of $181,000 and debts of $43,500.

WHAT THE SENATE HOLDS

The 1981 Senate is one of the richest in history—twenty-nine members are worth $1 million or more. One of them, John Heinz of Pennsylvania, lists nine holdings worth between '$250,000 and infinity.' Indeed, only five senators earn their total livelihood from their salaries. Major investments are in real estate, bank stocks, oil and gas companies, and defense-related corporations. The most prominent millionaires, largely of inherited wealth, are Lloyd Bentsen of Texas, Robert Byrd of Virginia, Dennis DeConcini of Arizona, John Danforth of Missouri, H. John Heinz of Pennsylvania, Edward Kennedy of Massachusetts, Russell Long of Louisiana, Claiborne Pell of Rhode Island, Charles Percy of Illinois, Dick Stone of Florida, Herman Talmadge of Georgia, and Lowell Weicker of Connecticut. Just about half of the millionaires are Democrats. Senators have a median net worth of $444,000.

BACKSTAGE IN CONGRESS

In 1979, Pasquale Bonnani, the chef in the kitchen of the House of Representatives, made $28,123. At the same time, the beautician at the House beauty shop, Kutley Hancock, earned about $7,800 plus tips. John Allen, the house barber, made about $4,000, plus tips. James Ford, the chaplain, made about $42,000, and James T. Molloy, the doorman, made over $52,000.

MONEY BAGS

Government employees who watch over the nation's money draw fairly comfortable salaries themselves. At the top is the Secretary of the Treasury, Donald Regan, whose salary is $69,630 (a significant step down from his previous job as head of Merrill Lynch, where he earned over half a million dollars per year); behind him is the Comptroller of the Currency, John Heimann, earning $55,388; and the third slot is filled by the Treasurer of the United States, Angela M. Buchanan, at $50,100.

FEDERAL JUDGES

Justice Warren Burger, of the United States Supreme Court, earns about $85,000 a year. For overseeing the United States Court of Customs and Patent Appeals, Howard T. Markey makes $65,000 a year. And Chief Judge C. Moxley Featherston of the United States Tax Court has a salary of about $61,000.

GOVERNMENT JOBS

There are 79,912 state and local governments, employing 13,102,000 civilians with payrolls totaling $13.4 billion. Over the last five-year period, employment rose 13.5 percent while pay rose 54 percent. In contrast, the federal government employs 2.9 million civilians with a payroll of $4.7 billion. For local civil servants, the national average salary works out to $1,227 per month, or $14,724 per year—before taxes. This compares with an average federal civil servant's pay of $16,206.

GOVERNMENT PAY

Public sector jobs employ one out of six workers, and periodically the question arises as to whether these workers are overpaid or underpaid. The average salary is in excess of $15,000. A post office window clerk, for example, earns $16,326 a year. Nevertheless, some federal civil servants earn as little as $7,000 per year, and at one recent point there were thirteen thousand government employees eligible for and obtaining welfare payments.

However, the debate goes on. It is generally agreed that upper-level professional and management personnel in government are underpaid compared with the private sector. But in a twenty-year comparison, from the mid-fifties through the mid-seventies, public civilian employees' earnings grew faster, 262 percent compared with 205 percent. Another study found that from 1960 to 1975, male federal employees had a 15 percent wage advantage and female federal employees a 21 percent advantage compared with employees in the private sector. This surge reflects an administration reform in 1962 to assure all federal workers pay comparable to those employed in private business.

Pay is not the only criteria: job security, working conditions, and social status must all be considered in evaluating compensation. However, in the area of fringe benefits, leave time, retirement programs, and steadiness of employment, federal workers enjoy an advantage. It is almost impossible to be fired: in a recent year only 223 people lost their civil service positions. Consequently, there are eleven applicants for every federal opening.

Nevertheless, fair pay in Washington is still a bone of contention. While the civil service does offer the security of a steady job, inflation has taken a steady toll in recent years, so much so that President Reagan had difficulty in drawing topflight administrators to Washington. The Federal Pay Advisory Commission, a nonpartisan body that meets every four years, recommended that the new administration of President Reagan propose raising the salary of the vice president from $79,125 to $120,000; cabinet officers from $69,630 to $95,000; members of Congress from $60,663 to $85,000; and substantial raises of $30,500 for district court judges.

On the other hand, members of Congress do receive sweet pension benefits when they retire or are defeated. They are paid 2.5 percent of the average salary earned in the three highest earning years in Congress and the military, multiplied by the number of years served. Other federal retirement benefits are added on. Thus, Frank Church, the defeated senator from Idaho, at fifty-four received $39,564 a year, and John Murphy, the Abscam-indicted representative from New York, also fifty-four, can soothe his pride with a pension of $31,512. Whereas Social Security beneficiaries have their payments indexed and adjusted to the cost of living as measured by the Consumer Price Index annually, past members of Congress have their pensions adjusted twice annually.

STATE PAY

While members of the U.S. Congress take home $60,663, state legislators are not so lucky. In New Hampshire they must make do with $100, but in California $30,767 is the annual pay. Across the country, the average pay for a state solon is $10,776.

Some states are perforce more generous, having instituted state lotteries to raise revenues. Though the odds are naturally with the "house," occasional winners do put a crimp in the take. For instance, Clyde Murphy hit the New York State lottery for $2,274,290, the biggest prize in any weekly lottery game in America. Even though the state has to pay off, they won't let Murphy have more than $50,000 a year.

BEST PAID GOVERNOR

Hugh Carey, governor of the state of New York and fourth husband of Evangeline Gouletas, earns $85,000 a year. He is the highest paid state official in the country. His new wife, a partner in one of the most successful real estate condominium conversion companies, has rapidly become one of the wealthiest women in the nation.

WHO'S WHO IN WASHINGTON TOILETS

Knowing who you're dealing with in complex bureaucratic Washington can be very important. Status means power. Power means perks. Thanks to the General Services Administration's guidelines, you now can have an insider's view. If the executive you meet with is sitting at a metal desk, then you're not even close to the front door. Wooden desks and chairs are reserved for those with a pay grade of GS-15 or above, meaning they earn at least $40,832 per year. If you notice a private toilet and sink, you're visiting an executive of level five through level one earning up to $69,630 annually. A toilet, sink, and shower means level one or two without question. And, if in addition there is a vanity chest, then you're with a for-real Washington "bigwig."

9

> If you want to know the value of money,
> try to borrow some.
> —BENJAMIN FRANKLIN

DEBT AND TAXES

DEBT AND DISPOSABLE INCOME

The average American is in debt to the tune of one-fifth of his/her disposable personal income. But for households in debt, repayments as a percentage of disposable income are close to 40 percent: that is, for families paying off mortgages, car loans, installment debts, and noninstallment debts, two out of five dollars go to paying off lenders.

On the average, Americans have piled up debts equaling one-third of their financial assets. Aside from the home mortgage, consumer debt is accounted for by the car (37 percent), personal items (18 percent), mobile homes (7 percent), home improvements (6 percent), bank credit cards (6 percent), bank credit (2 percent), and miscellaneous (24 percent).

PERSONAL BANKRUPTCIES

Last year, 355,000 individuals called it quits and decided to start over, via the bankruptcy courts. Under the present law, one can have the slate wiped clean once every seven years.

COMPANY FAILURES

Each year two million people think of starting a business, and 500,000 actually do. In the first two years, half of them fail. At the end of five years, almost 90 percent go belly up.

GOOD TRICK IF YOU CAN DO IT

According to an annual report of the National Advisory Council on Economic Opportunity, the households in the lowest 10 percent income group are spending 119 percent of their after-tax income on basics—food, housing, energy, and medical care. This deficit financing would, of course, be impossible if it were not for transfer payments, that is, moneys or services in kind that balance the budgets of poor people.

THE MARRIAGE TAX

The wages of sin or the price of virtue? Under the present tax laws, a married couple is taxed more heavily than a couple cohabiting without benefit of clergy. If a man and woman have a taxable income of $10,000 each, their joint tax is 2 x $2,097 or $4,194. But a husband and wife, each with a taxable income of $10,000, will pay $4,373 on a joint filing. The tax tribute amounts to $179.

At the $24,000 level, the cohabiting couple pays $6,799 each or $13,598. For the married couple, a joint return for $48,000 of income is taxed at $16,060. The marriage tax at this level is $2,462.

THE TAX TAKE

Nearly 91 million Americans paid $213 billion in individual federal income taxes in fiscal 1979—an average of $2,340 per citizen. This was an increase in dollars of 18 percent over the previous year. Individuals pay 45 percent, with corporations accounting for 15 percent, the remainder being paid by Social Security contributions, excise taxes, and custom taxes. Most taxpayers overpay through the withholding system: the average refund is $518. On the other hand, 3.4 million taxpayers underpay the government, an average of $234 per return.

MORE IS LESS

Back in 1964, the average family of four earning $8,132 paid 18 percent of its income in federal tax. By 1979, the average family, now earning $18,815, was taxed at 21 percent. Not only does progressive taxation, regardless of three rate cuts, push everyone into higher brackets, but also inflation reduces the value of money. The average family, fifteen years later, had lost over $1,000 in purchasing power. Furthermore, the actual tax rates for federal, state, and local taxes in the seventies jumped faster than the rise in goods and services, or the real output of business.

DISTRIBUTING THE TAX BURDEN

The overall tax system (based on sales and excise, payroll, income, property, and corporations) is progressive according to a study by the American Enterprise Institute. The top 15 percent of households pay roughly half of all taxes. Indeed, the top 10 percent contribute more than 40 percent of all tax receipts. On the other side, the poorer half of the population pays less than 15 percent of all taxes. In fact, the actual tax levies rise from 11.7 percent for the lowest 10 percent to 38.3 percent in the wealthiest 10 percent of households.

REVENUE SHARING

All taxes are created equal, but some are more equal than others. The federal government collects 58 percent of all taxes while the states collect 24 percent. Local governments collect the balance. When added together, all revenue authorities collected approximately $800 billion in the last fiscal year.

STATE TAXES

In 1977, just before the passage of Proposition 13 in California, state tax officials collected in excess of $10 billion. While a far cry from the federal tax bite, it does represent a per capita take of $472.18.

TAXING TIMES

According to the Tax Foundation, the average U.S. taxpayer worked until May 11 to pay his or her 1980 federal, state, and local taxes. Two years previously, the taxpayer had to work only to May 4. If the trend continues—a one-week increase every two years—by the year 2040 all your time will be spent working for the government.

THREE-MARTINI LUNCH

The IRS estimates that business people deduct up to $2 billion a year for meals and entertainment.

WHERE TO FLEE

State taxes were highest in Alaska (per capita $2,012) before the state abolished the tax, and lowest in New Hampshire ($298). Now the highest state taxes are in the District of Columbia and Connecticut. However, a study by economics professor Stephen Lile of Western Kentucky University found that low-income families were best off in Louisiana, while rich ones were best off in Florida. Southern New England states, New York, Pennsylvania, and Wisconsin are high-tax states at all levels of income. Florida, Louisiana, New Mexico, Nevada, Texas, and West Virginia are generally low-tax states. To put it in another light: New York is the worst state if you are rich and Massachusetts is the worst if you are poor.

In addition to the right state, it is important to flee to the right locality. Generally speaking, tax rates are lowest in small cities, ones with less than fifty thousand residents. And naturally, they are highest in the six largest cities of the nation. The average local tax burden across the country is $201 a year, but the burden in the cities is:

New York	$841.79
Philadelphia	389.57
Detroit	260.08
Los Angeles	239.47
Chicago	218.39
Houston	175.03

In small cities, the average local tax is $108.

10

It is plain madness to live in want
that you may die rich.
—JUVENAL

ALIMONY AND OTHER INCOME DISTRIBUTIONS

ALIMONY INCOME

The average alimony payment in 1975 was $2,895 per year according to the Tax Foundation. In Connecticut, the highest alimony state, the average payment was $9,728. North Carolina was the lowest, with payments averaging $954. Only 4 percent of divorced or separated women now receive alimony payments. Those who do are likely to be more than thirty years old, college educated, and have teenage children.

CHILD SUPPORT

Divorce and separation puts a great financial burden on most women: fully 28 percent of the 7.1 million mothers of children with no father present were living below the poverty level. Only 60 percent of separated mothers had been awarded or had an agreement to receive child support.

In general, child support payments account for 20 percent of the total income ($8,940) of women who receive such payments. The average payment was $1,800. Of the women who are supposed to receive child support, only 49 percent receive the full amount that is due them, 23 percent receive less than they are due, and the remaining 28 percent receive nothing.

By and large, women with voluntary child support agreements had average payments 50 percent higher than those with court awards. Only half of divorced women received any property settlement. For those who did have a property settlement between 1975 and 1979 the median value was $4,650.

FEMALE FAMILIES

Families maintained by women with no husband present increased by over 50 percent in the 1970s, the fastest rate of growth of any household units. Nor is it an urban phenomenon, since the fastest increases were in the suburbs. Children under eighteen years of age were present in 63 percent of the households. Of the women maintaining these families, 33 percent were divorced, 29 percent were widows, 21 percent were married with no husband present, and 17 percent had never married. Their median income was less than half that of all families—$8,540. Moreover, 31 percent of female-headed families live below the poverty level ($6,662), compared with only 5 percent for male-headed families.

THE AVERAGE FAMILY

The median family income, that is, the middle income and not necessarily the average one, in the late seventies was $17,640 when last measured by the Census Bureau. For white families it was $18,370, while for blacks $10,880—a difference of 69 percent. Hispanic families were somewhat better off than blacks, with a median income of $12,570. Farm family income was somewhat below the norm at $15,280. The level of poverty remained fairly constant throughout the seventies at 11.4 percent of the population. In order to qualify, a nonfarm family of four has to earn less than $6,662. Only 6.9 percent of white families are poor, while 20.4 percent of Hispanics and 27.5 percent of blacks live below the poverty line.

GIVE ME SHELTER

Homeowners with mortgages pay about 19 percent of their annual income for housing costs—mortgage, real estate taxes, property insurance, utilities. Naturally, costs differ with income levels: the rich pay less and the poor pay more in percentage terms. Households with incomes in excess of $25,000 pay only

13 percent, but those with incomes of less than $5,000 pay 35 percent of their incomes to maintain their homes. For households without a mortgage, the median income is $10,000, but $19,000 for households with a mortgage. The moral seems to be that the more one earns, the greater likelihood of mortgage debt.

Renters pay roughly 25 percent of their annual incomes for rent. Again the poor pay 35 percent of their incomes in rent, while the rich pay only 11 percent.

KEEP MOVING

American mobility is rooted in the frontier: it continues even though the frontier has vanished. Over a fifth of the nation's households move every year. Another way to look at the country's rootlessness is by noting the theory that everyone moves once in every five years. Of course, some people move three times, others not at all. Renters move four times more often than owners. Most people move for housing needs (39 percent), but also for family status (27 percent) and job reasons (22 percent). In the case of the transferred employee, automotive companies relocate personnel most frequently, followed by business machine makers and oil and gas companies.

TWO-INCOME FAMILIES

Married women, along with their unmarried sisters, have entered the labor force in extraordinary numbers. In 1965 only 35 percent of married women worked, but by 1980 over 50 percent of households had two salary checks. The median income for two-earner families is $18,704. Three-quarters of working wives claim to play an equal role in financial decisions. However, 15 percent say they make all the decisions, and only 8 percent leave money affairs entirely to their husbands, according to a survey of the Investment Company Institute.

CASTLE COSTS

The average price for a new one-family home in 1949 was $10,000. Labor and materials made up 70 percent of the purchase price while land accounted for only a little more than 10 percent. By 1979, the new one-family house sold for an average of $64,200. Labor and material costs shrank to 47 percent of the price of a home, while land costs soared to 25 percent. It was twice as expensive to finance a house in terms of percentages, but overhead and builders' profits went up only fractionally.

CITY-SUBURB GAP

The gap between city and suburban residents keeps growing; to wit, the people in the city are falling behind in earnings. In 1970, median family income of central city families was 83 percent of the income of suburban families. By the end of that decade, the city dwellers' income was down to 70 percent of that of their suburban counterparts. Moreover, suburbanites kept pace with inflation while city dwellers continued to lose purchasing power. In short, there is no evidence of any narrowing of the gap in spite of reports of middle-income families moving back to town.

INCOME AND INFLATION

The stable sixties were followed by the soaring seventies. Adjusting for inflation, family income in the sixties rose a hefty 34 percent, but hardly rose at all in the seventies—a modest 5 percent. The lack of real income increases was due to a stagnant economy that included two recessions and the increase in number of single-parent families (which have a lower family income). A family of four with a $10,000 income in 1970 would need $20,000 in 1980 just to stay even in current dollars.

THE INCOME PIE

Shares of the national income pie have remained remarkably stable since 1950. To put it another way, each quintile, or group of 20 percent of the population, has increased its dollar income but there has been no marked redistribution or movement from one group to another. In 1947, the lowest fifth received 5 percent of all income and the top fifth received 43 percent of all income. Thirty years later the distribution of the income pie was virtually the same.

At the end of the seventies, families earning $50,000 or more constituted the top 3.6 percent of the population, while families earning between $25,000 and $49,999 made up the next 24.3 percent. The subsequent 14.5 percent of households earned between $20,000 and $24,999.

The sources of personal income in the United States have also remained virtually the same over the last three decades.

Wages and salaries, plus other labor income, accounted for 70.7 percent of personal income, proprietors' income amounted to 6.6 percent, rental income 1.4 percent, dividends 2.9 percent, interest income 9.3 percent, and, finally, transfer payments by governmental agencies accounted for the remainder. The significant difference is that transfer payments doubled in the last thirty years, and interest income more than doubled, but proprietors' income fell nearly a third.

REGION BY REGION, STATE BY STATE

By the year 2000, regional income differences may have largely disappeared, according to the Advisory Commission on Intergovernmental Relations. Indeed, twenty years ago the per capita income of the five most affluent states was 85 percent higher than the per capita income of the five least affluent states. Today that income is only 47 percent higher. While the Pacific Coast states have replaced the Middle Atlantic states as the nation's wealthiest, the East South-Central and the West South-Central regions, the two poorest areas, improved markedly; but the East South-Central region (Tennessee, Kentucky, Alabama, and Mississippi) remains almost 20 percent below the national income average.

At the start of the eighties, the average national per capita income in the United States was $8,706. Alaska leads the nation with an average per capita income of $11,252, followed by Nevada with $10,204 and Connecticut, $9,959.

MINIMUM WAGE

First enacted in 1938, the Fair Labor Standards Act covered eleven million workers, requiring employers to pay a minimum wage of $.25 an hour. Since then it has been boosted fourteen times and now covers approximately fifty-two million workers. On January 1, 1981, the minimum wage rose to $3.35 per hour—an increase of 1,340 percent since its inception. In comparison, the Consumer Price Index rose fivefold.

While the minimum wage covers over half the work force, many people are not covered: civil service workers, the armed forces, employees in retail service businesses that gross less than a quarter of a million dollars a year, and workers on small farms.

Some states, such as Alaska and California, and the District of Columbia have rates that are higher than the federal level.

CLIPPING COUPONS

Not long ago the author Ferdinand Lundberg wrote in his book *The Rich and the Super-Rich* that nearly all the current large incomes "are derived in fact from old property accumulations, by inheritors—that is, by people who never did whatever one is required to do, approved or disapproved, creative or uncreative, in order to assemble a fortune." Not likely, and Lundberg offers no evidence to support this claim. Indeed, Census Bureau studies of the top 5 percent income earners show that a fifth of them are self-employed professionals and owners of small businesses, half are salaried professionals or managers, and the remainder are white-collar workers and others such as commissioned salespersons.

In a separate study, the Brookings Institution found that less than one-tenth of the very rich reported that more than half of their total wealth was from inheritance. Moreover, three-fifths of the rich reported no inheritance at all. At the pinnacle of wealth, a quarter of the super-rich reported that more than half of their current assets resulted from inheritance. Unlike the established wealthy classes of other nations, the upper income stratum in this country is relatively accessible. On the other side of the coin, there are no studies concerning the fall from economic grace, but Carnegie noted in the last century that it was but three generations from shirt-sleeves to shirt-sleeves.

FARMERS

One out of thirty-three Americans lives on a farm, about 6.5 million people in all, supplying an agricultural work force of 3.9 million. Farm families average $4,000 less in income than nonfarm families.

INCOME AND RELIGION

Although membership in a religious body does not preordain any level of income, there are marked denominational differences in earnings. These differences are due to a number of factors such as family background, educational level, geography, and, among others, dedication to the work ethic.

The National Opinion Research Center of the University of Chicago ranked (in 1974 dollars) non-Spanish-speaking whites as follows, based on a broad survey: Jews, $13,512; Episcopalians, $12,975; Catholics, $11,811; Presbyterians, $11,723; Methodists, $10,419; Lutherans, $9,725; and Baptists, $9,128. These figures are in line with the Census Bureau survey of 1957, the first and last government survey of denominational earnings: 25 percent of Jews had earnings over $10,000 compared with 8 percent of Catholics and 7 percent of Protestants.

TWO HUNDRED YEARS OF WEALTH

Comparing revolutionary America with the present, economic historians calculate that the net national wealth per capita has jumped seventeenfold. In 1775, per capita wealth was $1,550 (by 1975 standards) compared with $26,530 during the bicentennial year.

11

You'll get more gold
from men than from rivers.
—KURT WEILL/BERTOLT BRECHT,
Mahagonny

CRIME, PUNISHMENT, AND THE LAW

THE PRIME TAKE

In fiscal 1979, the number of bank robberies in the country rose to six thousand or one for every two and a half banks. This was an increase of 13 percent—just about equal to the inflation rate. T.G.I.F. has a special meaning to heist specialists since the Bank Administration Institute finds that 44.6 percent of all hold-ups take place on Friday.

TERRORIST PAY

From 1970 through 1977 there were 363 kidnappings of wealthy businessmen. A total of $146 million in ransoms was paid for the release of the victims, an average of $400,000 per incident. In 1979, there were over five thousand acts of political terrorism, increasingly aimed at multinational corporations.

BANK JOBS

Note jobs or oral demands reflect the amateurs of the bank robbery business, yielding an average of only $2,000 per event. Professional bank robbers, "over-the-top people," do much better, averaging $100,000 per job. On balance the occupation is relatively poorly paid: the FBI calculates that based on time served, the average bank robber's wage is far below the minimum wage of $3.35 per hour. (On the other hand, the cost to society is staggering since New York City authorities spend $71.87 a day, or over $26,000 per year, to maintain an inmate in one of its jails.) The exception to the rule was Stanley Mark Rifkin, who stole $10.2 million from California's Security National Bank in minutes by cracking its electronic transfer code.

SHOPLIFTING

A study of the police blotter of Washington, D.C., found that the average veteran shoplifter in 1971 was walking off with $30,000 worth of merchandise. By 1979, top shoplifters were stealing enough goods to earn them $53,000 a year. A cost-benefit analysis proves that the benefit is all on one side since almost no shoplifters are ever jailed.

HOT GOODS

Insurance companies in the 1970s paid out the most money for claims of stolen jewelry, followed in order by stereo equipment, portable television sets, power tools, guns, sports equipment, and silverware. However, the precious metals explosion at the beginning of 1980 caused gold and silver to zoom to the top of the list.

According to the law of averages, the typical American will fall victim to burglary twice in his or her lifetime. The average loss is $400 per theft.

WHITE-COLLAR THEFT

Service industries, which make up half of the Gross National Product, are particularly susceptible to crimes from the inside. Embezzlement and pilfering are responsible for a third of all crimes against business. They account for over $10 billion of losses: the hardest hit industries are cargo transport, financial institutions, and hotels and motels. Computerized crimes are the hardest to trace and the most devastating. Don Parker, a specialist in computer security, finds the average computer embezzlement to be on the order of $450,000.

DEATH AND TAXES

According to the old saying, the two inescapable facts of life in this vale of tears are death and taxes. However, ten Americans, including Walt Disney, have had themselves frozen, waiting presumably for a medical cure for their cause of death and a lower tax rate for their financial health before the resurrection. This cryogenic interment now costs more than $60,000, but without guarantees.

A number of Americans (the estimates range between 1.8 million and 9 million) participate in a netherworld in which their earnings remain unreported and their income untaxed. These "no-shows" come from all walks of life: the appliance retailer exchanging a washing machine for an artist's sculpture, a dentist fitting braces on the daughter of his house painter, the independent contractor who forgets to report the last job, moonlighters, the illegal alien, tourist, pensioner, and baby-sitter all working "off-the-books," and the whole criminal circuit, organized and unorganized, who prefer anonymity to a digital identity.

The IRS concluded that perhaps as much as $139 billion of income went unreported in the 1979 tax returns, income that would have generated at least $18 billion in taxes. Considering the fact that the federal tax bite is on the order of $213 billion, the government is losing 8 percent of its tax revenues. Other nongovernmental estimates place the size of the underground economy at between 10 and 27 percent of the Gross National Product, from $250 to $700 billion.

The recent explosion of this phenomenon stems from double-digit inflation, a Proposition 13 mentality, distrust of government programs, the inexorable tax squeeze from progressive taxation, and depreciation of the currency. Unless these issues are addressed, the underground economy may spell the death of America's "voluntary" tax system.

THE CRIMINAL CLASS

The most obvious tax evaders are the criminals. Even though their "earnings" may be wrongfully or fraudulently obtained, IRS regulation 1.61-14(a) insists that "illegal gains constitute gross income." Guesstimates suggest that between $25 and

$35 billion are gathered in criminal activities such as narcotics, gambling, and prostitution.

NONREPORTING

Most nonreporting of income comes from legitimate sources, that is, the income was earned in a legal fashion. Surveys find that the worst tax offenders are self-employed individuals with low incomes, incomes that are not subject to withholding taxes or information returns. Next on the hit parade are independent contractors—47 percent don't report anything. Self-employed small business persons do not report 36 to 40 percent of their incomes—especially if they deal in cash receipts. Rental and royalty income is also a major source of tax evasion: landlords, writers and composers, oil and gas tax-shelter participants drop 35 to 50 percent between the floorboards. Capital gains from sales of property or stock go unreported to the tune of 17 to 22 percent. Finally, 8 to 16 percent of dividend and interest income never sees a 1040.

One reason for the high rate of nonreporting is the odds against being caught. With only nineteen thousand revenue agents looking at 140 million tax returns and 500 million information returns, the likelihood of audit is not significant. In the tax lottery, only 2.63 percent of personal returns are seriously scrutinized if your income is between $10,000 and $50,000. If you make more than $50,000, the odds rise but they are still in your favor—10.4 percent chance of audit.

PROSTITUTION

Commonly thought of as the "oldest profession," prostitution is illegal in forty-nine out of the fifty states. The exception is Nevada. No one has ever conducted a census of prostitutes, but the work force is a sizable one if some metropolitan samplings are accurate. One estimate suggests that there are 200,000 prostitutes in the country, but it is not a figure vouchsafed by the Department of Labor. Another estimate guesses that the trade generates $10 billion a year, about what the country spends on jewelry and watches, or candy, annually.

Prostitution by and large is a transitory and peripatetic occupation (no pun intended) with an average work life of only three to five years. It is a young person's job: the typical age is closer to twenty than it is to thirty. The earnings of prostitutes vary from the lowly streetwalker found along highways, truck stops, and sleazy parts of town, to high-class madams whose earnings depend not so much on their own activities, but on the girls in their stables. The minimum price for the street hooker is usually $10 for oral sex (fellatio) or a hand job. A streetwalker will charge a minimum of $20 to accompany her client to a hotel, while the john is expected to pay for the hotel room. At the other end of the spectrum, hookers working the Waldorf-Astoria in New York or the Top of the Mark in San Francisco will make themselves $100 a trick. A prostitute's earnings are problematic at best: while she does not suffer from withholding and social security taxes, there is no certainty that she will be paid if her client is unhappy with her services. On the other hand, she must share part of the proceeds with the madam in a house or her pimp on the street. Consequently, it is difficult to arrive at a net earnings figure or an hourly pay scale for ladies of the night. Ms. Margot St. James, spokeswoman for a metropolitan trade association called COYOTE (Call Off Your Old Tired Ethics), claims that the average trick in New York is $45. During the Democratic Convention, demand overwhelmed supply and prices doubled. Ms. St. James reports that a female prostitute can earn $70,000 a year—about the going rate for a physician in general practice.

LAWYERS ON THE HILL

Because the government of the United States is so closely connected with the law, it is not surprising that so many people in public office were or are practicing lawyers. In the 97th Congress, almost half of the House members and more than half of the Senate hold law degrees.

Many derive outside income from lecturing and law practices on the side. A House rule now states that a member's outside income must be kept down to $8,625. This rule takes effect in the Senate in 1983.

BRIEF CASES

Politics is not the only field that those with a law degree, but not practicing law, go into. Because an awareness of the law is so important to big business, many companies have as their top executives people who have been trained in law. And, because these companies are such big money-makers, they are able to pay their most important employees accordingly. Irving Shapiro, past chief of Du Pont, earned $873,000. Ben W. Heineman of Northwest Industries makes $476,000. And Leonard Goldenson at ABC drew a yearly salary of $1,229,000.

LARGEST LITIGATION

Howard E. Minkie was involuntarily exposed to ionizing radiation in 1955 while in the army stationed at the nuclear testing grounds at Yucca Flats, Nevada. He claims that the exposure caused mutagenic defects in two of his children—one since deceased. Suing on behalf of himself, his children, a purported group of children with mutagenic defects who were born to army personnel so exposed, and the estates of these children, he is asking the government for damages in excess of $32 trillion. If granted, the damages would equal approximately the Gross National Product of the United States (at the 1980 level) for fifteen years.

12

Faced with economic policy decisions, Harry Truman sought the aid of professional economists. As they repetitively presented their "on the one hand," but "on the other hand," President Truman pleaded: "Will somebody please bring me a one-handed economist?"

LABORING UNDER INFLATION

INFLATION SCOREBOARD

As we all know, inflation takes a nasty bite out of our paychecks. As the rate of inflation varies, so too do the items affected by it. Many of us remember the three-cent postage stamp; who can forget it now goes for six times that amount? On the other hand, a few products remain relatively cheap: salt, for one, hasn't risen much in price in the last two decades. As the following list shows, the jump in prices was generally larger from 1970 to 1980 than it was during the previous decade.

Item	1960	1970	1980
1 dozen juice oranges	$.75	$.86	$.99
1 pound can of coffee	.75	.91	3.49
1 pound choice beef	.80	1.02	2.40
1 dozen eggs	.57	.61	.89
½ gallon milk	.47	.57	1.09
1 family house (new) with lot	16,700.00	23,400.00	64,300.00

Item	1960	1970	1980
4-door Chevy (Impala)	2,970.00	3,332.00	6,650.00
1st-class postage stamp	.05	.06	.15
Hospital room (semiprivate), daily rate	17.20	43.50	127.16
Funeral	732.00	1,075.00	2,085.00
Yacht: 40-foot power cruiser	41,990.00	69,900.00	157,400.00
Mink coat	5,000.00	4,000.00	6,000.00
Gold wedding band (14 K)	50.00	100.00	500.00

THE MIGHTY CPI

The most widely used government statistic, as far as income is concerned, is the Consumer Price Index. Using figures based on what consumers were buying in 1972–73=100, the CPI is made up of seven categories:

All items	100.0
Food and beverages	18.8
At home	12.2
Away from home	5.5
Alcoholic beverages	1.1
Housing	43.9
Rent, residential	5.6
Other rental costs	0.7
Homeownership	22.8
Home purchase	10.0
Financing: Taxes, insurance	9.2
Maintenance	3.7
Fuel oil, coal, bottled gas	0.9
Gas, electricity	3.4
Other utilities	2.2
Furnishings and operation	8.2
Apparel and upkeep	5.8
Commodities	5.1
Services	0.7

Transportation	18.0
Private	16.9
New cars	4.0
Used cars	3.0
Gasoline	4.2
Maintenance	1.5
Other	4.1
Public	1.1
Medical care	5.0
Commodities	0.9
Services	4.1
Entertainment	4.1
Other items	4.4

The index tends to be overly inflationary since it is based on the assumption that what people were buying they continue to buy at higher prices—especially energy. It also assumes that homeowners rebuy and refinance their houses every month. Another index, the GNP deflator, measures only what is produced and used, and is consequently thought to be a more accurate indicator of inflation.

Since millions of workers, retirees, and Social Security claimants have their income tied to the CPI, it is a closely watched and politically sensitive indicator.

THE COST OF LIVING GOES UP (CPI)

Year	Percent of Rise in Cost of Living
1960	1.5
1961	0.7
1962	1.2
1963	1.6
1964	1.2
1965	1.9
1966	3.4
1967	3.0
1968	4.7
1969	6.1
1970	5.5
1971	3.4

Year	Percent of Rise in Cost of Living
1972	3.4
1973	8.8
1974	12.2
1975	7.0
1976	4.8
1977	6.8
1978	9.0
1979	13.3
1980	11.2

WORLDWIDE INFLATION RATES (CPI'S)

	1978
United States	9.0
Switzerland	1.1
West Germany	2.6
Japan	3.8
Organization for Economic Cooperation and Development (an average of 24 member countries)	7.9
Britain	8.3
Canada	9.0
France	9.1
Italy	12.1

REAL MONEY

Actual disposable income per person rose by 17.5 percent between 1967 and 1973. From 1973 through 1978 the increase was only 5.5 percent. Since 1979, the numbers have been negative—a real loss in income. When adjusted for inflation, real discretionary income peaked in 1973 at $3,700 compared with approximately $3,000 in 1979. The diminished standard of living promised as a result of resource shortages in the seventies, especially oil, has come home to roost. Nevertheless, there will be no shortage of money. A congressional study projected that on the basis of yearly inflation (the modest single-digit type), family income is expected to average over $75,000 by the year 2000, and the IRS will take a tax bite of $11,351.

THE DISCOMFORT INDEX

Developed by the late Arthur Okun of the Brookings Institution, this index of pain is calculated by adding the unemployment rate and inflation rate together. When the total is over ten, the discomfort becomes noticeable; at twenty, downright unpleasant. Okun was the first modern economist to appreciate a new product of inflation—a stick with two short ends.

WORKING LESS

An A.F.L.-C.I.O. report, based on Bureau of Labor Statistics figures, asserts that office workers in Newark, New Jersey, have the shortest workweek. The average workweek, nationwide, is 38.2 hours, but in Newark the average is only 36 hours. In general, workers in the Northeast work the shortest weeks, while workers in the South put in the longest hours. Though the average is lower, plenty of Americans (45 percent) work a 40-hour week, a figure that has remained stable since 1948.

LABOR'S SHARE OF THE PIE

The price paid to labor as compensation for its services has risen slowly. Adjusted for inflation, labor's share of output amounts to 73 percent now, compared with 71 percent in 1956. Labor gets a smaller piece of the pie in Japan (56 percent) and Germany (68 percent), but considerably more in Great Britain (82 percent).

THE PRICE OF DISCRIMINATION

It is impossible to know the precise price of prejudice, but a Library of Congress study reports that it costs the country dearly. If the nonwhite population was as fully employed as the white population, and furthermore was paid an equivalent wage, $22 billion of wages and salaries would have been earned annually in the mid-seventies. If discrimination disappeared, at least against nonwhites, the total contribution would raise the Gross National Product by 3.7 percent or nearly $55 billion.

RACE WAGE GAP

Much progress was made since the 1950s in narrowing the wage gap between white and black workers. In 1955 black women earned only 57 percent of what white women earned, but by 1979 the difference had all but disappeared. This was not the case for black male workers. In 1955 they earned 63 percent of what white males earned, but only 75 percent by the end of the seventies, according to the Rand Corporation. At the current rate of progress, black men will not catch up to white wage earners until 2010.

PURCHASING POWER FOR PRODUCTION WORKERS

In the factories, production workers earned an average of $222.24 a week in 1977. Although this was a record in terms of current dollars, it showed little progress from the base year of 1967 if the dollars are adjusted for inflation and progressive taxation. Thus real spendable earnings for workers were $100 in 1967, but only $105.50 in constant dollars in 1977. Individual workers have prospered as they move up due to merit and seniority, but for a decade there was virtually no improvement, except for half a percent a year, in the ranks of labor. Since 1977 average hourly pay has risen from $5.50 to $7.50 in 1981, but inflation has all but robbed the increase of any additional purchasing power.

EMPLOYMENT VERSUS UNEMPLOYMENT

In 1978, there were 99 million workers in the nation, of which only 6.5 million were unemployed. Economists consider the economy fully employed when 4 percent of the work force is unemployed. Another way of looking at the idea of full employment is to measure the number of people working against the working-age population. In the full employment years of 1956 and 1966–69, the average was 56 percent. In 1981, the percentage of the working-age population employed reached a record 60 percent.

UNITED STATES LAGS AS PAY LEADER

For years the United States was the leader in the international league when it came to salaries. No longer. According to a Conference Board study, in the mid-seventies Denmark, West Germany, Switzerland, Norway, and Belgium all passed the United States in beginning salaries for engineers. (Engineers were used as a basis of comparison since their job functions are very similar in the surveyed countries.) But due to depreciation of some foreign currencies, the purchasing power of the dollar moved the United States up to fourth place for number of hours worked to purchase major appliances.

UNION VERSUS NONUNION PAY

Manufacturing industries that move from an unorganized status to unionization increase their wages by about 10 percent according to a study by the National Bureau of Economic Research.

EMPLOYMENT AND SELF-EMPLOYMENT

For all the talk about being your own boss, rugged individualism, and the pursuit of independence, over 90 percent of the American work force is employed by someone else. Only in Great Britain are there more wage earners and salaried workers (92 percent). In contrast, Spain, Ireland, and Italy have the greatest proportions of their labor forces as employers, self-employed, or unpaid family workers.

PAID VACATIONS

A Swiss bank compared the number of paid vacation days given to secretaries and plant managers around the world and across the country. New York averaged two weeks of paid vacation for secretaries, Chicago three, and the West Coast, about two and a half weeks. In Madrid, secretaries had thirty days of paid vacation, the highest amount, with Canada and the United States the least generous. For plant managers Düsseldorf offered twenty-eight days, and Dublin fifteen days—the best and the worst records. In the United States, plant managers had an average of three weeks as a paid vacation.

GETTING TO THE JOB

Fifty million Americans commute to work—85 percent travel by car or truck, 6 percent use public transportation, 5 percent walk, and 1 percent go by motorcycle or bike. The remaining 3 percent never leave home. The average commute to work is nine miles and usually takes twenty minutes to complete. Car and truck drivers take nineteen minutes to get to work, while public transit users spend an average of forty minutes.

THE NIGHT FRONTIER

Increasing numbers of Americans are working nights—and not in bars or bordellos. Eleven percent of the work force is now occupied in such nocturnal jobs as data processing, transportation, printing, and a slew of other production jobs in industries that have moved to a twenty-four-hour schedule. While the graveyard shift used to be a dead end for marginal workers, the new emphasis on night work finds that there is a 6 percent shift premium in wages.

RETIREMENT YEARS

Back in 1950, a working man could look forward to 5.8 years out at pasture. Today, the golden years for men retiring at sixty-five last for fifteen years and five months. Women can look forward to living to eighty-five.

SOCIAL SECURITY VERSUS AVERAGE PAYMENT

Due to an 11.2 percent increase in the Consumer Price Index in the last twelve months, Social Security pensioners will receive a comparable boost in their monthly checks for the next year. The average payment for 1981–82 is $374 a month. The minimum for a covered retiring worker is $153.10, and the maximum payment for a retired worker is $653.80 ($980 if married to an elderly spouse). For an elderly couple, average Social Security benefits are $563 per month.

In addition, a pensioner over sixty-five but less than seventy-two can earn up to $5,000 without suffering any reduction of Social Security benefits. Beyond that level, payments are reduced $1 for every $2 earned, no matter what amount is earned.

FUTURE BENEFITS

The new Social Security law passed in 1977 greatly reduces prospective benefits, especially for low-income workers. Under the old law, low-income retirees could look forward to benefits equaling between 52 and 63 percent of their final average earnings; middle-income from 32 to 51 percent; and upper-income from 21 to 46.7 percent of final pay. However, in the year 2000 a worker now earning $10,000 will receive 48 percent of his last five years' average pay; $20,000 employees will receive 32 percent; $30,000 employees will receive 23 percent.

THEN AND NOW

In 1940, when the first benefit checks went out, 228,000 people received a maximum of $41.20 per month. In 1979, 34 million recipients received benefits totaling $102 billion, for an average of $3,000 per beneficiary, compared with the first benefits that averaged only $153 per year.

ONE-THIRD OF THE NATION

Based on the 1980 Census, the Commerce Department has found that one out of three American households receives help from the government. Out of the 79 million households, 27 million obtain assistance from one of the following five benefit programs: Medicare, Medicaid, food stamps, school lunch, or subsidized housing.

HOURLY PAY: HOME AND ABROAD

In the 1960s the United States had the highest wage scales in the industrial world. In the seventies all that changed as American pay gains slowed to a crawl while foreign workers managed to achieve hourly gains and keep inflation from gaining on them. Compensation in manufacturing in 1978 almost made the United States look like a source for cheap labor:

	Per hour
Belgium	$10.18
Sweden	9.93
Netherlands	9.88
West Germany	9.41
United States	8.26
Canada	7.44
France	6.80
Italy	6.17
Japan	5.41
United Kingdom	4.29

HOLY SEE'S SALARIES

The highest paid members of the Vatican are the cardinals, with a salary of $982 a month. At the other end, clerks and manual workers receive $145 a month, plus a cost-of-living allowance of $368. Meanwhile, estimates of Vatican wealth range from $275 million to $1 billion.

COMPARATIVE STANDARDS OF LIVING

The real Gross National Product per person, according to the World Bank, at the time of the bicentennial placed Switzerland first and Romania last:

Switzerland	$8,877
Sweden	8,673
United States	7,894
Canada	7,512
Denmark	7,450
Norway	7,424
West Germany	7,380
Belgium	6,781
France	6,552
Israel	3,923
USSR	2,759
Romania	1,793

However, standards of living are not easy to compare and certainly encompass more than economic output and annual income. The United Nations and the University of Pennsylvania created an index based on purchasing power parity, a method of comparing currencies' domestic buying power, rather than the usual exchange-rate equivalents. Based on 110 consumption categories, the United States far and away exceeded the industrialized world's per capita consumption of goods and services. To put it in concrete terms, the standard of living in the United States (100 percent) exceeds that of its nearest contenders, France (68 percent) and West Germany (66 percent), when measured by such items as the number of telephones, cars, televisions, and flush toilets per population.

DISTAFF DOMINANCE FAR OFF

Although there are 5.5 million more women than men in the United States, it is still a man's world as far as work is concerned. However, the picture is changing. In 1960, only 10 percent of the nation's families had a woman as the chief breadwinner. By the end of the seventies that figure rose by 40 percent, with 14 percent of households headed by women.

UNEQUAL PAY

In June 1978, women in the work force passed the 50 percent point, up from 43 percent in 1970. Though there are far more women working than there were a decade ago, the Census Bureau finds that the differential in the median income of women compared with that of men remains the same. The latest figures reveal that men made an average of $15,070, and women $8,810—a gap of 59 percent. The lack of progress in achieving equal pay for comparable work, even though mandated by the 1963 Equal Pay Act, is due to state "protective laws" (which keep women from taking jobs with risk of injury), lack of education, low-level entry into the labor force, and, of course, sexual discrimination. One estimate suggests that it would cost $2 billion a year to close the gap.

Beyond the issue of unequal pay, women simply work harder than men. Reiterating that old rhyme that "men work from sun to sun, but a woman's work is never done," a report from the Worldwatch Institute found that in twelve countries women worked (including housework and child care) an average of 70.2 hours a week. Men, on the other hand, worked only 60 hours. Finally, the institute found that work patterns in Communist countries were roughly the same as the rest of the world, in spite of the abundance of day-care centers there. In the last analysis, equal pay and opportunity may be, in the words of the institute, "a recipe for overwork."

WOMEN'S WORK

The Bureau of Labor Statistics has categorized the women's labor force in the following ways:

Clerical	35.0%
Service	11.2
Professional and technical	16.1
Machine operators	11.5
Sales	6.9
Managerial and administrative	6.4
Private household service	2.6

Craft	1.8
Nonfarm laborers	1.3
Farm	1.2
Other	6.0

WOMEN OF WEALTH

Although women are making some notable advances in senior management, only 3 percent of those earning more than $25,000 are women. This figure is higher in large cities; in New York, for example, it reaches 10 percent.

The situation is similar for women business owners (whose numbers are increasing): they represent about 5 percent of all U.S. businesses, but less than .5 percent of annual receipts.

In the professions women are making their fastest strides. In law over 9 percent of practicing attorneys are now women, compared with only 2.8 percent in 1970. The situation is similar in medicine: today close to 10 percent of the practicing physicians are women.

$

PART TWO

The Going Rate

13

> There is hardly anything in the world that some men cannot make a little worse and sell a little cheaper, and the people who consider price only are this man's lawful prey.
>
> —RUSKIN

INDUSTRIAL PRODUCTION

ALUMINUM WORKERS

Aluminum, once considered an exotic metal with limited use, is now behind only iron and steel in production and usage. Aluminum products range from household appliances and cooking utensils to automobiles, aircraft, and missiles.

Three-fourths of the workers in the aluminum industry are production workers. The plants are located near sources of alumina and abundant electricity, which is essential to the making of primary aluminum. Alumina is refined from bauxite ore and most plants are situated in Arkansas, Louisiana, Texas, Alabama, and Tennessee, where the ore is mined (some is imported from the Caribbean islands) and where electricity is available through developments like the Tennessee Valley Authority.

The production process is not dissimilar to the production of iron and steel in that it involves furnaces, movement of raw materials, filtering out the desired aluminum, and disposal of various useless residues.

Most production workers are hired as unskilled workers and get their training on the job. As workers gain skills and seniority, they are usually moved into more responsible and better paying jobs. Many companies have craft apprenticeship programs, usually lasting from three to four years, and most professional jobs require a bachelor's degree in science or engineering.

Alumina plant workers average more than other workers in manufacturing industries, from $8.75 to $10.00 per hour. Indeed, they are considered to be in the highest paid industry in the manufacturing sector. Fringe benefits are very good. Skilled operators and maintenance and craft workers hold the highest paying jobs in the plants.

Employment in the industry is expected to keep pace with the average of all manufacturing industries and may even grow faster as new uses for the versatile metal are discovered and developed.

THE APPAREL INDUSTRY

The apparel industry employs some 1.3 million people in this country, almost 80 percent of them engaged in making clothes. Insiders often affectionately, and sometimes not so affectionately, refer to it as the "rag" business. The mass production of apparel requires creative people, management personnel, and production workers. More than half the people in the industry are production workers doing hand sewing or using sewing machines.

Typical jobs include:

Designers: A designer has an idea of what an article of clothing should look like, whether it be a ball gown, a business suit, or a pair of pajamas. He or she usually makes a drawing of it and then cuts out pieces of cloth that are pinned and/or sewn together on a mannikin or a model until the clothing matches the sketch. A good designer usually earns between $25,000 and $60,000 a year. There are no hard and fast rules. In the rarefied atmosphere of high society and high fashion, a designer can make millions; that is, if you are a Coco Chanel, an Yves St. Laurent, or a Pierre Cardin. Rare birds.

Sample Makers: They take the designer's creation and make a one-time sample of it, completely sewn together in appropriate fabrics. If the management approves, the sample is then used to make patterns and garments are created on a mass production scale. Sample makers usually acquire their skills on the job. Base pay is $5 to $7 an hour; in many plants sample makers receive additional compensation for the number of pieces they do.

The Sewing Room: Most people in the sewing room are women operating electrical sewing machines and being paid on a piecework basis. Sewing-room workers have been averaging between $3.50 and $4.00 an hour, an estimated 30 percent below the average for all other production workers. Requirements for these jobs are minimal and training is on the job.

Tailors: Tailors are specialists in the apparel industry. They do the most difficult hand and machine sewing. These craftsmen are customarily employed in the creation of expensive garments, and, depending upon whom they work for, their salaries will vary, but $6.90 per hour is about average.

The apparel industry is very sensitive to general economic conditions. Clothing is both a necessity and a luxury. People cut back on buying luxury clothes as soon as money gets tight.

AUTOMOBILE WORKERS

The United States is a country of mobility, and Americans love to drive. A Californian thinks nothing of making a three- or four-hour trip to visit some friends. A New Yorker spends three hours a day battling rush hour traffic going to and from work. But not only do Americans love to drive, they also love their cars. They're proud of them and spend a lot of time and money caring for them.

It's no surprise that the motor vehicle industry employs more workers than any other manufacturer, but it is astonishing that new cars are driven off the automotive assembly line at the rate of about one a minute. One out of every hundred workers is involved in the production of motor vehicles, while many more jobs have been created by the industry—motor vehicle repair shops, automobile dealerships, gas stations, and highway construction, to name a few.

There are approximately three thousand auto manufacturing plants producing everything from small parts to diesel trucks. Two-thirds of the jobs are in Michigan, Ohio, Illinois, Wisconsin, and western New York; Michigan leads the group with its famous Motown. In fact, 40 percent of the total number of auto workers are in the Great Lakes region.

Workers in this industry can be divided into three groups—designers and engineers; parts production workers; and assemblers, finishers, and inspectors.

Designers and Engineers: Sometimes they design custom-made bulletproof cars for heads of state, fully equipped with telephone, television, and a bar. And sometimes they plan the new body of a sleek sports car streaked with silver stripes and black flames. But more often than not, designers and engineers work on ideas and models for new cars and trucks that will be appealing, useful, and safe for the millions of Americans who drive.

Automotive designers are usually graduates of an art institute or a school with a strong art department offering a major in industrial design. Engineers need at least a B.A., and they often have higher degrees that give them more experience in research and development of ideas. In many instances automotive companies provide financial aid for designers and engineers to further or update their education. Starting salaries vary between $10,000 and $14,000 a year, while experienced industrial designers can earn over $30,000 a year.

Parts Production: One-quarter of the workers in the automotive factories are machinists, tool and die makers, mechanics, and supervisors. These are skilled jobs that take at least four years of training. Although some learn on the job, most are trained in apprenticeship programs offered by the manufacturers and unions. Experienced machinists earn an average of $8.51 an hour. There is a marked regional difference in hourly earnings: in San Francisco, Oakland, Detroit, Houston, and Chicago the rates are close to $10.00 an hour; in Jackson (Mississippi), Boston, and New Orleans the rates are roughly $7.50 per hour. In addition there are many benefits, including in some cases supplemental unemployment payments during layoffs.

Assemblers, Finishers, and Inspectors: An assembly line worker can usually learn his/her job in a few hours because it is so repetitive in nature. Finishers and inspectors obviously need more training and experience, but in both cases their skills are learned on the job.

More sophisticated mechanization is expected to replace some of these jobs over the next decade. In fact, even now an industrial robot can do tasks such as welding body panels and feeding parts into machine tools. Meanwhile production workers earn an average of $10 an hour with time and a half for overtime and Saturdays; paid vacations, insurance, and holidays; and annual wage increases. The unions are strong and have fought to provide coverage for workers during layoffs and slow periods.

BAKERS

If civilization is measured by the quality of its bread, as some contend, then American society peaked in the late 1950s when the country employed a record number of bakers—ninety-six thousand. Today there are only seventy-nine thousand (rather fewer bakers than dentists), earning an average $5.98 an hour or $233.22 for an average industry week of thirty-nine hours.

Most bakers work in large automated bakeries that employ "continuous mix" machines. Consequently, the jobs in a bakery are quite specialized: mixers, divider machine operators, dough molders, bench hands, and oven tenders. In small bakeries, the all-around baker performs most of the tasks, from mixing to icing. An all-around baker is paid between $5.66 and $8.19 an hour. While baking is a good, steady industry—it does not experience the contractions and expansions of the economy since demand is relatively constant—computer-controlled baked products have reduced the need for bakers. On the other hand, it appears that there will always be a market for original baking and fancy pastries. In addition, the Bakery and Confectionery Workers Union will always need a president: the present one is Harold Friedman, a baker who reportedly earns $337,182 from all his union positions. Some dough!

BLACKSMITHS

"Under the spreading chestnut tree" the chestnuts are getting deeper and deeper around the empty anvils. The village blacksmith, once as vital to country life as the doctor, is seldom seen. The few who remain have moved for the most part into factories and mines.

Of the approximately ten thousand working blacksmiths, almost two-thirds are employed by the railroads, factories, and mines at hourly wages ranging from $6.00 to $10.76. The remainder work in small shops and are mostly self-employed.

Many beginners start as helpers while others enter formal apprenticeships that usually last three or four years. These programs often lead to jobs as forge operator or hammer operator. Farriers (blacksmiths who specialize in shoeing horses) either learn by assisting experienced farriers or take a three-to-four-week course that is taught at several colleges. Farriers handling saddle horses earn from $15,000 to $20,000 a year, while those specializing in racehorses may make up to $25,000 annually. The outlook for industrial employment is expected to go down through the mid-1980s, but the number of farriers may increase slightly due to the growing popularity of horse racing.

BOILERMAKERS

Boilermakers are the real sculptors of America's urban industrial skyline. They—along with the layout workers who design them and the fitters who make the parts—have built the giant storage tanks, vats, valves, tubes, and stacks that stand as the symbols of the modern industrial world.

Most boilermakers belong to unions, principally to the International Brotherhood of Boilermakers, Iron Shipbuilders, Blacksmiths, Forgers, and Helpers. Although union wage rates average $11.55 an hour (compared with $10.63 for all building trades), the industries that employ boilermakers are especially sensitive to economic conditions, so layoffs can be expected. The highest wages are in the petroleum industry, and the lowest in railroad work.

BOOKBINDERS

The ancient craft of bookbinding—consisting of leather tooling, embossing, and hand folding—is practiced almost as rarely in our time as it was in medieval days. Although a few of these creative artisans remain out of the total of eighty thousand bindery workers, working in conditions not unlike the monk in his tower, most books are now put together in noisy, machine-filled binderies. Workers perform a single mechanized routine task, such as folding printed sheets into units called signatures or assembling these units in order.

Since the machines that accomplish these tasks are ever more fully automated, jobs for factory binders are steadily being eliminated. Pay is less than that of other printing crafts. Experienced bookbinders average $8.55 an hour. Wage rates for bindery workers are among the lowest for the entire printing industry at $5.78 an hour.

COAL MINING

Coal, once one of this country's most vital commodities, was eclipsed by petroleum until soaring oil prices in the seventies reawakened interest in America's huge coal resources. Coal mining is now enjoying something of a renaissance, employing 233,400 miners at an average salary of $20,000.

Today's coal mining teams operate sophisticated machinery rather than wielding picks and shovels. In addition to the workers who run the actual mining machine, mines employ mechanics to keep the machines in order, fire bosses to inspect for hazardous conditions, rock-dust machine operators, roof bolters, stopping builders, fitters, carpenters, and many others.

How many jobs will actually be available in coal mining over the next twenty years depends on a number of factors still too uncertain to predict. Certainly, there will be a need for coal to produce electricity and to assure America's energy independence. How much can be used will depend on several factors: the price of alternative energy supplies, the speed with which coal gasification and liquefaction can be developed, and the environmental questions raised by strip mining and air pollution resulting from the burning of high-sulphur-content coal. While demand for mining is likely to remain strong, it remains the most dangerous industry in the country.

DRUG MANUFACTURING

Though Baeyer and Squibb in the nineteenth century were the first to develop the lowly but ever-present aspirin, pharmacologists are still not sure precisely how it works. Most of the modern drugs, of which there are about ten thousand, are better understood, since they must be extensively tested. The scientists, engineers, and technicians—especially the chemists and biologists—are the backbone of the industry. However, five out of six jobs in this industry are held by white-collar clerks, administrators, and production or processing workers. Production workers are paid a little better than the $7.50 per hour made on the average by manufacturing workers.

Job opportunities exist in drug companies that are doing research in genetic engineering—an area bound to expand in coming years. For instance, Genentech, a new company doing work on insulin and interferon through gene splicing, became a public corporation and made its two founders (one a biochemist) instant millionaires fifty times over.

ELECTRONICS MANUFACTURING

The electronics bonanza started in the early 1900s with the crystal set. By 1930, the radio industry had grown to include television. But World War II really expanded and diversified electronics manufacturing. Military needs led to the development of radar, air flight control equipment, and the digital computer.

Today it is an enormous industry, producing thirty thousand different kinds of finished products for government, industry, and the home, and employing 1.3 million people. A big part of electronics manufacturing (one out of every nine jobs) is still research and development: the extension of existing knowledge of electronics and the application of these newly discovered principles to an endless array of real products and processes. Besides jobs for physicists, chemists, metallurgists, mathematicians, statisticians, and electronics engineers, there are many less obvious professional careers. For example, industrial designers must create attractive, functional containers to hold all those complicated innards. Technicians are needed to back up the engineering and design efforts. Technical writers and illustrators are needed to prepare training and user manuals. And some electronics products are so complicated that it takes an engineer to sell them. Indeed, sales engineering is the most lucrative part of the industry, with salesmen often working on a commission basis.

Making these products is complicated and requires hordes of skilled and semiskilled workers. There are special needs for glassblowers and glass lathe operators to make tubes, and for grid lathe operators to wind fine wire around two heavy parallel wires to make the insides of tubes. And there are special electronics processing jobs. For example, electroplaters and tinners, anodizers, silk-screen printers, and etching equipment operators are needed. So are operators of infrared ovens and hydrogen furnaces, exhaust operators, and sealers—all of whom deal with the special problems of making vacuum tubes. Assembling telephone and telegraph apparatus is the highest paying part of production work, at $6.73 per hour.

IRON AND STEEL WORKERS

The iron and steel industry employs over half a million people in more than nine hundred steel plants in the United States. There are over two thousand job specifications in the industry, and about 80 percent of all workers are engaged in moving raw materials and steel products within the plants and maintaining the machinery that processes iron ore. If you can't stand the heat get out of the iron and steel business, since furnaces are synonymous with the trade. But keepers of such furnaces earn $8.48 per hour. Most other production workers earn more with the average wage in the industry at $9.41 per hour, and the workers operating the hot strip mills earn $10.54 per hour. Jobs in the industry are scarce since it is suffering from overcapacity and foreign imports; nevertheless, the head of United States Steel earns $360,000 and the chief of Bethlehem has a base salary of $460,000.

LOGGERS

Such is the primeval forest today that most loggers live at home and commute to work. A fallen tree may be removed from its site by a heavy-duty helicopter, or even a balloon. And what felled it in the first place is likely to be a giant pair of scissors called a tree harvester that cuts timber four times faster than a saw.

A typical logging crew consists of five to fifteen workers. A forester selects and marks the trees to cut. The faller and buckers fell the marked trees and then cut them into manageable pieces. Then a choker setter puts a giant steel noose around each piece and attaches it to a tractor that "skids" the log to a landing. A rigging slinger supervises the loading. In rough terrain, a yarder engineer may operate a winch that acts like an enormous fishing rod and reel and hoists the logs onto the landing. In very tight spots, the helicopters move in. Once the logs reach the landing, a loader engineer operates a machine that picks them up and puts them on a trailer, which is then conveyed by truck or railroad to the sawmill.

Most of the ever-declining number of jobs in the logging

industry are clustered in the West and the South—46 percent in Oregon, Washington, California, Alabama, North Carolina, Arkansas, and Georgia. Wages are higher in the West, but pay varies with the task. West Coast fallers and buckers earn more than $10.60 per hour, while choker setters make $7.66. Employment is not seasonal, but it is sensitive to recessions, when construction generally slows down. Use of machinery has cut overall employment in logging by half since 1950, a trend that continues. Jobs related to running and maintaining the machinery may increase, and there should also be good prospects for forestry technicians involved in conservation.

MACHINE MOLDERS/FOUNDRY WORKERS

Most foundry workers are either pattern makers or core makers, or molders, but there are many minor specialties. Traditionally, casting was done by hand, but today machines are taking over. The trend is for large, highly mechanized foundries that produce great quantities of identical castings and employ fewer workers.

Although conditions in many foundries have improved, pouring molten metal is dangerous and workers are inevitably exposed to heat, fumes, and dust. They are also exposed to sporadic unemployment, since this industry responds to variations in the business cycle. The pay scale is slightly above average for manufacturing jobs, and higher for iron and steel than for nonferrous foundry workers. Production workers earn $7.64 an hour, compared with $6.48 in nonferrous foundries.

MACHINISTS

Machinists are those highly skilled craft workers who combine a knowledge of all types of machine tools with an understanding of the properties of various metals. This enables them to figure out how to make a metal part that will do almost anything. They work from blueprints and specifications, select the right tools and materials, plan the cutting and finishing operations, compute dimensions, supervise production, check accuracy, and polish the various elements with hand files before assembling them into the finished product.

There are currently about 400,000 machinists working in electrical, transportation, fabricated metal products, and other consumer industries, earning an average of $8 an hour, an annual salary of $16,600.

MILLWRIGHTS

Most of the ninety-six thousand millwrights in this country work for manufacturing companies, installing the heavy equipment used to make metal, paper, lumber, and other products. There are hazards in this work, despite hard hats and safety belts, but the wages are a third higher than average—ranging from $9.48 per hour in Indianapolis to $8.56 in Chicago and $6.74 in Boston.

PHOTOENGRAVERS

Nobody writes sonnets about Easter bonnets anymore, and it's equally unlikely that you'll find that "you're in the rotogravure." The parade is passing by the old photoengraving shop as cheaper, faster offset lithography replaces the traditional letterpress and gravure techniques for most of the nation's printing.

There are eight thousand photoengravers, compared with nearly thirty thousand lithographers, and the gap is expected to widen in coming years as more and more of the major book, magazine, and newspaper publishers turn to offset. Still, there will probably always be a market for wedding announcements and special high-quality books that warrant the use of elegant printing techniques. Those who work at this delicate and demanding craft earn an average of $9.63 an hour.

PRINTING PRESS OPERATORS

There are 145,000 press operators and assistants, mostly working for book, magazine, and newspaper publishers. Others work in banks, hospitals, insurance companies, and government agencies. Press operators are trained in an apprenticeship program, but there are long waiting lists for entry into the program and people often work at unskilled tasks for several years before they can enter training. Press operators go through a four-to-five-year apprenticeship; their assistants must complete two years of the combined classroom and on-the-job training.

Most pressmen belong to a union and receive union hourly wages. Newspaper press, in-charge operators receive the highest wage, a minimum of $9.32 an hour, while book and job cylinder press operators receive $8.77 and their assistants earn $7.72. Workers on night shifts receive higher wages.

PROJECTIONISTS

The projection booth is about as far behind the scenes as you can get in the movie business, but it's not a bad place for those who love flicks and don't mind privacy. This is not the most convivial job in the world, but it isn't the most difficult either, especially with the new, automated equipment that takes the tedium out of reel changing.

Most up-to-date projection systems are preprogrammed (by the projectionist) to do everything from dimming the lights and pulling the curtain to switching and rewinding reels. On the other hand, for those who find romance in the split-second repair of broken sprocket holes—generally undertaken to the accompaniment of hoots, whistles, and stamping feet—the small-town or neighborhood theater still offers a challenge. In these traditional setups, the projectionist works continuously throughout the screening, changing twenty-minute reels and alternating two projectors so that as one reel finishes, another begins without perceptible interruption. The more mundane tasks of cleaning and maintaining the equipment, and shipping back the film, are part of all projectionists' jobs.

Little advancement is possible in this work, and there is not much prospect for further growth in the job market. TV continues to cut into the motion picture theater trade, and the trends toward automated equipment and multiscreen theaters will also hold down the number of jobs available for projectionists to about eleven thousand total jobs. While the beginner earns $5.18 an hour, the average going rate for an experienced projectionist is $12.50 an hour.

TEXTILE MILL WORKERS

Spinning and knitting mechanisms have become so complex that computers and machinery are rapidly taking over many of the jobs formerly done by the human hand and eye. Still, there are a million Americans working in the seventy-two hundred textile mills and factories today. Textile workers, on the whole, are not well paid. Their average hourly pay of $4.29 compares poorly with the $7.50 average in all manufacturing industries.

One-quarter of all textile workers are paid according to how much they produce, but the majority receive hourly wages. In addition to low wages, textile workers often work long hours—forty-six to forty-eight hours a week. Because mills run twenty-four hours a day there are three shifts. Despite the unfavorable aspects of their jobs, only one-fifth of all textile workers belong to unions that can arbitrate grievances and protect workers from layoffs.

TOOL AND DIE MAKERS

The 180,000 tool and die makers work in major manufacturing areas of the country. One-fifth are in Detroit, Chicago, and Los Angeles. They may work in large plants that produce machinery or in smaller shops that do subcontracting work for major industries.

These versatile machinists can be trained in apprenticeships, vocational schools, or on the job. The four-year apprenticeship programs provide training on many machines including the drill press, lathe, grinder, and milling machine, as well as classroom work in mathematics, shop theory, tool designing, and blueprint reading. Skilled tool and die makers can advance to supervisory positions in industry, become tool designers, or open their own tool and die shops. Because they have a knowledge of a variety of operations, they can change jobs more easily than most machinists, and because of their skills they are among the highest paid of all machine workers. Their wages range from $7.19 to $10.53 an hour with fluctuation based on the area of the country in which they work. San Francisco/Oakland is the highest while New York and Chattanooga are at the low end of the scale. There is a general shortage of skilled tool and die makers throughout the country, with thousands of jobs going unfilled even in the midst of the last recession.

14

The banks are just as greedy
as everybody else.
—WILLIAM MCCHESNEY MARTIN,
Chairman of the Federal Reserve System for nineteen years

OFFICE

ACCOUNTANTS

Counting other people's money is the heart of the accounting profession, and being richly compensated is the result. Every year over sixty thousand accountants enter the field, starting work with an average salary of $16,956. Most accountants work for industrial companies, keeping a nine-to-five schedule along with their co-workers. Some work for government agencies, perhaps as IRS agents or bank examiners. Only 29 percent of new accountants will be employed by independent accounting firms.

Life with the "Big Eight," the major public accounting firms, is profitable indeed for partners and principals. For example, at Peat Marwick (the nation's largest firm), the senior members of the company average over $115,000 per year, and junior partners earn $55,000. The ex-chairman, Walter E. Hanson, is considered the superstar of the industry—in one recent year his gross compensation reportedly exceeded $804,000. His replacement, T. L. Holton, receives over $900,000. Other superstars did almost as well: Harvey Kapnick of Arthur Andersen & Co. earned $526,000 and John C. Biegler of Price Waterhouse & Co. earned approximately $400,000. Some sums!

ACTUARIES

People who are good at figuring odds may become successful gamblers or speculators, but someone who loves a sure thing may prefer the security of being an actuary. Actuaries calculate risks for insurance companies. They assemble and weigh the latest statistics to come up with a fair price.

The first five or ten years finds them studying twenty-five hours a week for the many examinations they must pass on their way to fellowship in the Society of Actuaries. Salaries rise by $500 to $850 following each exam they pass. Eventually an actuary can become a top executive with "the ear of the king" in directing company policy. Most work for private insurance companies in New York, Hartford, Chicago, Philadelphia, and Boston. Top actuarial executives average $47,600 a year.

BANK OFFICERS

Today's banker deals in printouts instead of penny rolls and offers customers a long list of special services. As banking becomes more sophisticated, there is a greater need for well-trained managers to hold down costs and maintain efficiency.

Banks employ over 300,000 officers—presidents, vice presidents, controllers, loan officers, trust officers, electronic data processing managers—and a myriad of department heads specializing in international finance, inter-bank relations, and community affairs.

Although the promising clerk is occasionally promoted, most supervisory jobs are filled by management trainees hired right out of college. A Master of Business Administration degree capping a bachelor's degree in social science is ideal training, worth $1,400 to $1,600 a month to start. A graduate with a B.A. in finance or liberal arts, with emphasis on economics and accounting, may be hired at $900 to $1,100 a month. Branch managers in medium-sized banks earn $25,000, but department heads in large banks will earn between $40,000 and $60,000 per year. Banking is not as well paid as comparable jobs in manufacturing. However, the top three banks pay their leading men rather well: A. W. Clausen, before he left BankAmerica for the World Bank, earned $709,085; Walter B. Wriston of Citicorp, $639,000; David Rockefeller of Chase Manhattan, $618,000 before his retirement.

BANK TELLERS

As long as cash flows, bank tellers will be needed to give, take, and keep track of it. There are currently about 310,000 full-time tellers, earning from $95 to $175 for a thirty-nine- or forty-hour week. Head tellers, after years of experience, may earn as much as $1,200 per month. Finally, a head teller may become an assistant cashier, the leading noncommissioned officer in the bank, so to speak, and earn $1,500 or $1,600 per month.

BOOKKEEPERS

There are currently nearly 1.8 million bookkeepers at work, earning an average salary of $724 a month, with experienced accounting clerks averaging $916. This is not a glamour job, but it is a secure one since the accountant and manager depend on the resulting information. Bookkeepers had better love numbers—or money—or both. General bookkeepers in small firms may perform a variety of balancing and calculating acts during the day, but those who work for large offices tend to specialize in one kind of routine task, preparing a daily income statement, or feeding accounts receivable and accounts payable information into the computer.

The job outlook is mixed. While it is a large field with many jobs and high turnover, actual employment growth will be slow through 1985, and slower thereafter due to increasing use of data processing machines that are generally more accurate and economical than human calculators.

CITY MANAGERS

How to keep the buses on schedule, negotiate with the police, allocate funds for the schools, get rid of snow, garbage, crime, air and water pollution—and still find time to run for reelection? Many mayors and city council members are solving this problem by hiring a professional—or a whole set of professionals—to run the city while they make policy. Although some big cities have them, most city managers work in towns of under twenty-five thousand. Most of the three thousand city managers are employed by cities and counties that have a council-manager system, but some work for mayor-council systems, too.

As cities become more complex—and complexity is one thing we can count on for the future—more managers will be needed to untangle things. The job requires management skills, diplomacy, good public speaking, a familiarity with accounting, and patience with bureaucracies. Salaries for city managers range from $22,000 in cities of ten thousand inhabitants to more than $50,000 in cities of over a hundred thousand, and competition for these jobs is heavy among the more than nine thousand management assistants who are already hustling their way up.

CLAIM ADJUSTERS

When your house burns down or your car is damaged in an accident, you want a rapid and fair settlement from your insurance company. Justice—with speed—is the particular challenge of the claim adjuster.

The claim adjuster (there are about 169,000 of them) is a person on the go, with a company car and a travel expense account. Claims investigation may take the adjuster to remote parts of the country to interview witnesses and claimants at the scene of a hurricane, fire, crime, or accident. Calls often come on weekends or in the middle of the night. The average salary for this peripatetic job is $14,760.

COMPUTER OPERATORS

Someone may tell you that you get your weekly paycheck from a computer or that your hotel reservation has been made by an electronic registrar. In fact, these machines may facilitate all kinds of organization, but they still need operators to tell them what to do.

Keypunch operators, data typists, console operators, and high-speed printer and converter operators all work directly with putting information into the computer and receiving the output. Keypunch and data typists record, by way of a typewriter keyboard, the pertinent data on cards or magnetic tapes and disks. Console operators put the cards or disks into the computer and watch it to be sure it runs correctly. High-speed printer and converter operators translate output that emerges in a language other than that desired by the client. Sometimes these operators are assisted by a tape librarian who catalogs the many pieces of information that a single computer can handle.

Many of the 565,000 computer operators learned most of their skills on the job. High schools, vocational schools, private computer schools, and business colleges offer computer training that provides valuable background for understanding electronic equipment, but each business has its own way of setting up data and organizing its computer system. The federal government, for example, accepts applicants with special computer training and experience even if they don't have high school diplomas. Console operators have the most difficult of these jobs and need several months of training before they can find the cause of computer breakdowns. These operators also have the greatest possibility of advancement—sometimes moving into supervisory positions or jobs as programmers.

The rapid changes in computer technology are decreasing the demand for keypunch operators, who in fact have one of the more repetitive, often tedious tasks. Keypunch trainees earn between $160 and $185 a week while those with experience earn $220 to $250. Console operators earn $160 while learning, then $200 to $260 depending on experience and ability. All computer operators have the option of working any one of the three eight-hour shifts. No one can afford to turn these expensive machines off at night.

COURT REPORTERS

Court reporters have to be able to take words in through their ears and simultaneously let them flow out through their fingers. Every word of testimony and examination has to be taken down accurately for the official transcript of the proceeding.

Court reporters are highly skilled stenographers, and they have usually completed a special two-year course in shorthand reporting. In addition to learning the ability to record very quickly, they also need some legal background so that they can follow the jargon of the courtroom.

In fourteen states court reporters must pass an examination to become a certified shorthand reporter (CSR) before they can record legal proceedings. Another title, considered the highest in the profession, is that of registered professional reporter (RPR). This is awarded to candidates who pass a two-part examination and continue their education in related programs.

Shorthand reporters in the courtroom generally work with a stenotype machine that allows them to record faster than handwritten stenography. The federal government requires that they be able to take 175 words a minute while many other employers require more than 225 w.p.m. Sometimes shorthand reporters work as free-lancers and record out-of-court testimony for lawyers and meetings. Others record the proceedings of the U.S. Congress, state assemblies, and meetings of government agencies. Shorthand reporters earn an average of $1,000 to $1,400 per month. The federal government pays between $876 and $1,085 a month with rates based on speed, educational background, and experience.

LAWYERS

President Carter took note that our legal system, with "expensive talent on both sides," nevertheless left the country "overlawyered and underrepresented." Certainly justice is expensive, but only partly due to salaries of lawyers. Legal salaries range from $10,000 to $30,000 based on experience, field of specialization, and employer. New lawyers average between $15,000 and $18,000, except for the relative few who start with Wall Street firms where the starting salary now exceeds $35,000. On the other hand, legal aid and public service practitioners start with as little as $10,000, and experienced federal attorneys earn an average of $24,308. In short, lawyers on straight salaries receive less compensation than is usually thought to be the case. Attorneys employed by in-house legal departments of major corporations earn an average of $35,000.

However, three-quarters of all lawyers practice privately, earning an average $55,000 per year, second only to doctors as a group in overall compensation. Partners in large law firms, of course, make much more since top attorneys such as Sargent Shriver of Field Frank Harris Shriver & Jacobson in New York or Leon Jaworski of Fulbright & Jaworski of Houston charge consultation fees of $250 per hour. The practice of corporate law is most lucrative since the rewards come not only by the hour but also sometimes on a contingency basis, that is, a percentage of the recovery if there is one. The largest recovery to date was made by Jenner & Block of Chicago, which successfully represented MCI Communications Corporation against AT&T in an antitrust suit. If the judgment of $1.8 billion is upheld, the law firm will make a record fee of $93 million.

There are over 500,000 practicing attorneys in the country. Prospects are not encouraging with a glut in New York and California.

SECRETARIES AND CLERICAL WORKERS

"Raises! Not Roses!" is the new cry of the secretarial pool. The heightened consciousness of secretaries and clerical workers is likely to increase pressure for better pay in the 1980s. The work force of 3.6 million secretaries would certainly welcome any change since the average clerk typist in large cities earns between $7,500 and $9,000 per year. Certified secretaries earn somewhat more with the average yearly salary close to $13,000.

There is a general shortage of secretarial help, and a skilled secretary with experience is able to negotiate a substantially better salary. Due to the overwhelming demand, men have entered the trade in force, filling 5 percent of the jobs. Other changes have also made the work more exciting: the "office of the future," with electronic word processors, facsimile telecopiers, intelligent typewriters, and smart photocopying and transcribing machines, has created a demand for skilled help. This translates into higher salaries for those with special training.

At the upper echelon, executive secretaries may earn $350 to $500 per week. However, at that level they are being paid for their administrative abilities, not their secretarial talents.

TRAFFIC MANAGERS

Whatever it is, wherever it's going, getting it there is the job of a traffic manager. These people, more than twenty-one thousand of them, bring in the raw material and deliver the finished goods on time. In a literal sense, they keep American industry—and consumption—moving.

Traffic managers exist at several levels. The humblest prepare bills of lading, trace lost shipments, and figure freight charges, for which they are paid less than $10,000 a year. More experienced managers take a creative role in the company's operations, arranging schedules with production and purchasing department personnel, and choosing among many possible modes (rail, air, road, water, pipeline, or a combination) for moving goods. People at that level earn about $10,000 a year. At the highest level, a traffic manager may make policy decisions and even represent the company before regulatory bodies such as the Interstate Commerce Commission. The going rate for that job is about $19,600 annually.

15

Prosperity is more than an economic
condition, it is a state of mind.
—FREDERICK LEWIS ALLEN

SERVICE

BARBERS/HAIRSTYLISTS

About half of the 121,000 barbers in the United States operate their own businesses. Those barbers who have specialized in such services as hairstyling and coloring are called hairstylists. Some barbers have chosen a simpler route by removing their white jackets, replacing them with flowered sport shirts, and doubling the prices of their haircuts.

All states require licenses, and, although qualifications vary from state to state, a person must generally have completed the eighth grade, pass a physical exam, and be at least sixteen (in some states eighteen) years old. Barber training is offered in about 350 schools; 3 out of 4 schools are private. Programs usually last nine to twelve months. Replacement needs for the profession are high compared with other professions.

The shift from simple haircuts to more personalized services has had a great effect on the occupation, and those specializing in hairstyling have been more successful. The result is that opportunities are greater for hairstylists than for regular barbers. For those considering going into their own business, new equipment for a one-chair shop costs from $1,500 to $3,000.

BARTENDERS

To be a good bartender, it is not really necessary to be a psychiatrist. It helps, though, to have steady nerves, a strong back (to lift beer kegs), and enough manual and mental dexterity to mix twenty-five different drinks in half an hour and to remember regular customers' nuances of taste. Bartenders must be at least twenty-one.

Bartenders are in it for varying reasons. Some like to work part-time or odd times; many travel between summer and winter resorts. One out of five are self-employed. This is a learn-on-the-job profession, although courses are available in some cities. Many beginners start out in the neighborhood bistro or sign on as a bartender's helper in a large establishment. Most jobs are in the big cities of the big states, with New York and California leading the list. The average pay ranges from $3.34 to $6.53 an hour, plus tips that average at least 50 percent of their pay, and sometimes as much as 100 percent.

BEAUTICIANS

The queens of ancient Egypt were buried with their combs and cosmetics—and sometimes an unlucky beautician or two. The beauty business is safer these days and still flourishing. Barbershop trade declined in the mid-seventies, but beauty shops are thriving, with a total of 542,000 beauticians employed. The projection is uphill through the eighties, as more women work and more men patronize unisex shops.

Every town has its beauty salon, but the hairstylists who set fashion trends are in New York, Los Angeles, and other fashion centers. The pay is better in the big cities, too. One Hollywood hairdresser charges $200 for a first visit and "consultation." But most beauticians can expect to make between $330 and $390 per week, including tips.

All states license beauty operators. The examination consists of a written and a practical test of beauty skills from haircutting to permanent waving. In some states a separate exam is given for manicurists. Private daytime and evening courses are available in most cities, and take about a year to complete. Many vocational high schools also offer cosmetology along with academic subjects.

BUILDING INSPECTORS

Building inspectors work for city and suburban building departments, with employment concentrated in regions undergoing rapid growth. Unlike other construction-related jobs, there is little seasonal variation. Salaries range widely, based on experience, specialization, and locale, running from $14,000 to $22,000 a year. The West has the highest average salaries and the South has the lowest. For the government, salaries range from $13,000 to $19,000 a year.

The work is physically demanding with a lot of ascending and descending of building-in-progress, plus hours of traveling (usually in a company car) between work sites. Entrance to the profession is via previous experience as a construction contractor or craft worker. Intensive knowledge of a specialized area, such as electrical or plumbing systems, reinforced concrete, or structural steel, will help in getting a job.

CIVIL SERVICE

The federal government is the nation's largest employer. Uncle Sam's time sheet covers nearly every job known in the private sector—plus a few (like internal revenue agent) that are unique to government service.

The main difference between being a clerk typist (or even a biologist for that matter) for the federal government and being one in private industry is in the open hiring process. The merit system covers 90 percent of all federal jobs. This means that jobs are awarded on the basis of an individual's experience and examination scores rather than according to political opportunity. Once hired, the government worker steps onto an automatic wage escalation and grade promotion track that—assuming he or she achieves seniority without being caught in a departmental budget cut—makes for ironclad job security, with excellent benefits, straight through to retirement.

Although some are employed by Congress and the courts, most federal employees work for the executive branch. This includes (among other departments) all of the armed services, the Post Office, and the Veterans Administration—three mini-empires unto themselves. There are approximately 2.8 million civilians employed by the federal government—2 million of them white-collar workers.

The biggest single occupational group in the government is general clerical workers. Nearly a million of these secretaries, telephone operators, and mail and file clerks work throughout the government.

Engineering is another big job category. Two-thirds of the approximately 150,000 positions are in the Department of Defense. Next largest is accounting workers—120,000 of them spread through Defense, Treasury, and the General Accounting Office. Hospital, medical, and public health personnel are another large group, working primarily for the V.A. and the departments of Defense and Health and Human Services, and Education.

Transactions with the private sector, such as purchases and distribution of supplies, account for another substantial slice of the government employment pie. Significant numbers of workers are also to be found in law, social science and economics, biology and agriculture, investigative and inspection work, mathematics, and the physical sciences.

Entrance requirements obviously vary according to profession and department. A high school education generally qualifies an applicant for trainee jobs in technical or clerical work. Junior college or technical school degrees raise the entry-level salary. Four years of college or responsible job experience is required for administrative and managerial grade levels, and a professional occupation demands a college degree in that field or equivalent work experience. In all cases, judgments as to qualification for specific jobs are made according to the rules, and the test results, by experienced personnel people in the U.S. Civil Service Commission, which operates 62 area offices and 100 Federal Job Information Centers throughout the country.

Blue-collar workers are less conspicuous than white-collar bureaucrats, but still account for substantial numbers in every government agency. In 1980, over half a million of them worked in navy shipyards, ran mobile equipment, chauffered senators, baked and served apple pie, changed light bulbs, and printed government documents. Many of them without previous training got jobs by applying to one of the government apprenticeship programs and passing a written examination that rated their learning potential as good. Those with more experience could apply for a position at the journeyman level.

Postal Service: The mail is a monumental, moving mass, coming and going everywhere at all hours, despite the proverbial weather problems and the newer hazards of computer breakdowns. Trying to hasten it along are 680,000 mail carriers, mail handlers, postal clerks, technicians and mechanics, postal inspectors, postmasters, and line supervisors, right up to and including the postmaster general himself. Most of these civil servants work in or out of the corner post office or at one of the more than three hundred regional mail processing centers.

Anyone who aspires to a job with the postal service must pass an examination for the specific job he or she wants. Vocabulary and reading ability are important aptitudes for most postal employees, and the mail handlers' exam also requires physical proof of the ability to lift a seventy-pound sack of mail.

The postmaster general, who presumably is not required to lift a seventy-pound sack of mail, is one of the best paid civil servants, on a par with cabinet secretaries, earning $69,630 annually. At the other end, a new full-time mail carrier starts his career at $14,603. Most of the carriers earn an average of $17,168. For part-time work, around the holiday season, carriers may earn $7.27 per hour, plus 10 percent more if they work nights.

COOKS AND CHEFS

Professional cooks and chefs prepare everything from the ordinary double-whammy hamburger to a $250-a-person French dinner at the Palace Restaurant. Some cooks specialize in salads while others are experts in sauces. Some perform on TV and others only come out of the kitchen to meet their audience under great pressure. A few are artists, most are merely competent, and the rest dangerous to your palate.

More than one million Americans work as cooks and chefs (outside their homes) and their ranks are expected to increase over the coming years as more people dine out more often. Depending on the size of the restaurant or institution, a cook may work alone or he or she may work with several other cooks as well as assistant cooks and helpers. Nowadays cooks are also assisted by very capable kitchen machines like the food processor and the microwave oven.

Most cooks learn on the job. They may work in a fast-food

restaurant or an institutional cafeteria or the armed services peeling potatoes and chopping onions. Others are trained in vocational schools, colleges, or apprenticeship programs. Students in professional cooking programs take most of their classes in a kitchen since you can't learn to cook from a book. The most creative cooks, upon whose talent the reputation of a restaurant depends, can earn more than $40,000 a year and sometimes share in the profits. Perhaps the most prestigious chef in the country runs the White House kitchen; for his efforts Pasquale Bonnani is paid $28,123 per year. However, the majority of cooks earn between $3.35 and $6.36 per hour, depending on the class of restaurant at which they work. Assistant cooks earn slightly less and chefs earn slightly more. But it's not unheard of for a star chef at a first-class restaurant to make $40,000 or more a year.

FARMERS

The best way to get a farm these days is to inherit one, preferably a big one. Unless you want to grow mushrooms or some other intensive farming crop, it's impossible to compete with massive corporate and family farms that use mechanized systems to cultivate thousands of acres. Almost nobody can afford to buy this much land anymore. In fact, with more than 1.5 million acres of farmland turning into suburbs each year, it is becoming almost impossible to get started in farming except as a tenant farmer on somebody else's land, or as a farm manager.

Running a farm is just as hard as getting one. Farmers work long hours in the growing season and need the strength of Ulysses, as well as his patience. These days, the farmer also needs the management skills of a corporate executive. Whether he or she owns the farm or rents it from somebody else, the farmer must plan carefully and economically, planting a judicious combination of crops so that bad weather or price fluctuations won't wipe out the entire year's profit. Loans must be secured for buying machinery, fertilizer, livestock, feed, or seed, depending on the type of farm it is. And whatever the final product—cotton, tomatoes, heifers, or buttermilk—it must be gotten to market or storehouse safe, fresh, and, the farmer hopes, at the moment when the price is right.

Nobody knows how much the average farmer earns in the

average year. Prices vary dramatically, and a farm that shows a large profit one year may show a loss the next. In 1970 the average farmer had an income of $4,800; in 1975, $8,845; and in 1978, $10,434.

All this may still not deter those who, like Miss Scarlett, have an irrational love for dirt. If that is the case, the next best training to growing up on a farm is to take two to four years of post-secondary training at an agricultural college.

FARMHANDS

There are two kinds of farmhands: those who get paid and those who are part of the family. There are 975,000 of the former and 340,000 of the latter. Cesar Chavez notwithstanding, the family workers are generally better off.

Some farmhands work on dairy and crop farms, using their hands relatively rarely, except to shift gears on the hay baler, or to pat old Bossie on the flank while a machine does the repetitive tasks. On some large farms, there are highly specialized jobs (for example, irrigators do nothing except control the water supply). Workers who care for livestock may have a quite varied daily schedule: feeding, watering, cleaning stables, and caring for the health of their animals. Workers on crop farms perform different chores in different seasons.

A third of all hired (nonfamily) farm laborers work in Texas, California, and Florida, growing, picking, and packing vegetables and fruit. And, although a tough-skinned tomato has been developed permitting machines to handle this formerly handpicked crop, many fruits and vegetables still require the services of migrant day laborers. As dozen of films and television documentaries have dramatized, these workers are among the hardest working and the lowest paid in the nation. The average wage of all hired farm workers is only $3.25 an hour compared with $7.50 for workers in private industry. Although they occasionally receive room and board allowances plus a bonus, almost none receive health or other typical benefits.

FARM MANAGERS

Today's trend toward superfarms has brought about a new kind of farm employee. Neither a farm owner nor tenant farmer, but far more than a supervisor of hired workers, the farm manager heads up a large corporate or partnership farm, running the business end and planning and scheduling all of the various farm enterprises. Many farm managers are employed directly by the corporation or partnership. Some work for businesses that specialize in supplying management services for absentee landlords, and some are self-employed. Earnings vary greatly, usually starting at $15,000, but incentive pay can add substantial compensation.

Less than a quarter of all farms are run by farm managers, but, because of the way large farms are taking over the market, this is the only farm job that shows real promise for the future for aspiring 4-H-ers who don't have a farm in the family. These young people should attend an agricultural college and then go looking in one of the states where farm management positions are concentrated.

A third of all farm products are raised in Iowa, California, Texas, Illinois, and Kansas. The Plains States (Kansas, Nebraska, Iowa, and Illinois) grow the most wheat, corn, and other grains. The rolling hills of Wisconsin, Minnesota, and New York invite grazing dairy herds. And the South is the only region that can sustain crops like cotton, tobacco, and peanuts, which have long growing seasons.

FBI/CIA

Even if thousands of American boys and men are tantalized by the glamorous adventures of James Bond, there are, alas, very few openings in these two agencies. There are only eight thousand FBI agents and most of them won't be giving up their jobs—they're career positions with required retirement at age fifty-five if they've served at least twenty years.

The FBI is part of the U.S. Department of Justice and it has jurisdiction in areas of federal crimes such as bank robberies, kidnappings, white-collar crime, organized crime, espionage, and conspiracy. The CIA is an entity unto itself; recent public and government discussion has revealed that no one knows exactly what its jurisdiction is beyond gathering foreign information. Ostensibly, its tasks are more of a fact-finding nature.

An applicant for the job of FBI agent must either be a graduate of a state-accredited law school or have a college degree in accounting. (These agents investigate embezzlements and fraud in violation of federal laws.) A few applicants are accepted with degrees in science or a foreign language or with three years of specialized experience related to the FBI's work. All applicants must be between twenty-three and thirty-five years of age, physically strong, and have excellent hearing and vision with natural color perception. They also need to be willing to move anywhere in the United States or Puerto Rico. Strict physical, written, and oral examinations are given before a candidate is accepted and even then appointments are probationary for one year. New agents are trained for fifteen weeks at a U.S. Marine base in Virginia. Following that they work for two weeks with an experienced agent before going on independent assignments.

The starting salary for an FBI agent is $17,532, with periodic raises based on satisfactory performance. Upgrading of position brings a higher annual earning. Supervisors start at $32,442. Most agents work more than a forty-hour week with overtime of up to $4,400 a year.

FIRE FIGHTERS

In early times, the fireman kept watch over the town from a perch high up in a fire tower, and if smoke was seen, he rang a bell to summon volunteers who would then race the horse-drawn fire engine to the burning house. There are still motorized versions of the volunteer fire company in many small towns throughout America. But most big cities and metropolitan areas have paid, professional fire fighters—an increasing number of them women.

Fire fighters may specialize in rescue, ventilation, and salvage, in the operation of fire apparatus, emergency rescue vehicles, or fireboats, but most are trained in all rescue skills, including first aid. Between alarms fire fighters polish a lot of chrome and brass, stretch miles of wet hose, inspect buildings, and take part in community education programs.

Applicants for municipal fire-fighting jobs must meet certain height and weight requirements and pass a written test and medical examination. Those who pass with the highest marks are then sent to fire school where they learn the techniques and practice drills. Needless to say, courage and a sense of public service are as essential as physical strength and endurance. Despite safety procedures, each job entails an inherent risk of death and permanent injury that cannot really be compensated for by disability insurance and pension plans. Depending on the size of the city, the average fireman's wage ranges between $15,000 and $18,000.

FOOD COUNTER WORKERS

The hardest thing about this job is learning the jargon, which flies faster than flapjacks and is frequently colorful. "Burn one, two over easy, Adam and Eve on a raft." Food counter workers deal with short order cooks—in short order. Sometimes they also are the short order cooks, doing everything from taking customers' orders, cooking, making sodas and sundaes, and cleaning the grill, to sweeping up and carrying out the trash.

More likely today, the counter worker stands behind a microphone and a computerized cash register in one of the big nationwide fast-food chains. These fast-food emporiums often hire young people who are still in high school as part-time workers. They may also operate formal management training programs for their experienced full-time personnel who show leadership ability.

Promotion opportunities are generally not great in this field. Most job escalation is in the form of transferring to a larger restaurant, or possibly becoming a fountain or line supervisor. Although this is one of the worst-paying jobs in America—wages range from $1.70 to $3.73 an hour—some counter workers make a fair amount in tips, and nearly all get their meals free—if they can stand to eat what they've been serving all day. Jobs are easy to find and will remain plentiful.

GUARDS

Guards who work in large office buildings make sure that IBM Selectrics don't walk out the door at night. Guards in museums watch carefully to see that no one touches the paintings and sculpture. Guards at a baseball game help prevent the crowds from rioting with enthusiasm, and guards in banks—well, they've had a couple of bad years lately.

Nearly all large institutions, offices, factories, and transportation facilities need guards to patrol for vandalism, fire, and theft. Today 550,000 people work as guards, and more jobs will be opening each year. Some employers look for guards who have had experience in military, state, or local police departments. The federal government hires only veterans who have also had some experience guarding. Obviously, guards need character references and clean records.

Many guards work for security agencies that send them out to various assignments. Others have steady employment in public and private situations and their wages vary accordingly. The average hourly pay is $3.63, but those in transportation receive $5.29. Those in service industries, including the security agencies, earn $3.10. Two-thirds of all guards are night owls and they may receive a higher salary for keeping their eyes open when it's dark.

INSPECTION AND MAINTENANCE WORKERS

Once products are put together, they must be tested. Inspectors are employed by the thousands. Some inspection jobs require years of production and technical experience, particularly those involving missiles, spacecraft, and computers. Other inspectors simply stick one tube after another into a metered testing device.

The machines employed in electronics manufacturing may be almost as complex as the electronic systems themselves, and must be maintained rigorously. Repairs require highly specialized knowledge and training.

Because of the variety of products and processes, and of the jobs involved in making them, it is difficult to suggest how salaries run in the industry as a whole. In fact, pay scales vary with the complexity of the inspection or assembly job. The highest paid inspectors are those who test components and subassemblies in complex products like missiles, and who help make experimental models for the military and various industrial uses. These workers earn well above the scale for comparable jobs in other industries. Yet some electronics assemblers earn less than the average for other types of manufacturing. Workers who put together radio and television sets, and those who make component parts, are below scale. Wages for inspectors vary from $3.85 to $8.68 per hour.

Like salaries, employment opportunities vary and may be expected to fluctuate unpredictably from year to year because of economic and political events that determine defense spending. There will probably be more jobs for skilled maintenance workers and inspectors, simply because of the extraordinary number of products being turned out and sold each year. On the other hand, the employment opportunities for assembly workers and testers will rise more slowly because of increased use of mechanization and automation.

INSPECTORS: OCCUPATIONAL SAFETY AND HEALTH

Some twenty thousand barrels of toxic chemical waste ignite and explode in Elizabeth, New Jersey, sending a dangerous black cloud over Staten Island. During the Christmas rush, a young postal worker is caught by the gears of a large mail-loading machine and crushed. A nuclear technician misreads signals from a reactor, an automatic safety device fails, and an entire nuclear plant nearly melts down. We hear about only these dramatic episodes. Other ongoing environmental and occupational hazards like poor ventilation in factories that use potent solvents, continued exposure to high levels of microwaves, and the use of pesticides that may cause organic damage in humans are perhaps more threatening to the general population's well-being.

Health and safety inspectors working for both the government and private industry are continually monitoring and regulating products and practices that will affect the public. In many instances they are successful; in others the job becomes just too politically and bureaucratically complex for them to be effective.

Health inspectors are government employees. They work in several areas: food and drug, meat and poultry, agricultural quarantine, and environmental health. Although the U.S. Food and Drug Administration may set many of the regulations in these areas, most health inspectors work on a state and local level in checking factories, stores, and restaurants for proper processing, labeling, and storage. Environmental health inspectors also monitor waste disposal and air and water supplies.

Government regulatory inspectors work in a broad range of fields checking to see that government rules and standards are followed in immigration, customs, aviation, mining, wage-hour compliance, alcohol, tobacco and firearms, and occupational safety.

Safety engineers work in large plants identifying possible hazards and devising systems to prevent accidents. They also maintain checks to make sure that the final product is safe for the consumer.

Fire protection engineers specialize in possible situations like *The Towering Inferno*, and the handling and storage of flammable products.

Industrial hygienists eliminate on-the-job hazards like excessive noise, lint, fumes, asbestos or metal particles, radioactivity, and water pollution that may threaten workers' health.

The government employs a hundred thousand health and regulatory inspectors, while only twenty-eight thousand work for private industry. Employment in both sectors is expected to grow in the eighties with the increased use of new chemical and organic substances that could be life-threatening on a mass scale.

Training required for inspectors varies with the area in which they work. For many positions, the federal government requires a bachelor's degree or three years of related work experience and a passing grade on the Professional and Administrative Career Examination (PACE). Federal aviation inspectors must have experience in aviation maintenance as well as pilot certificates and flight experience. Environmental health inspectors need a bachelor's degree in the field in which they specialize, and in thirty-five states they are licensed by an exam. Private industry often prefers safety and health workers with graduate-level training in industrial hygiene or occupational safety engineering. In addition they hire people with two-year-college degrees as technicians. All safety workers continue their education while they are working to learn how to handle new technologies and products. The Occupational Safety and Health Administration (OSHA) is active in these on-the-job training courses.

Government inspectors start at between $10,507 and $13,014 a year depending on their position and qualifications. Aviation and mining inspectors are exceptions, with starting salaries of $14,097. Experienced government inspectors earn between $14,000 and $24,000 a year with meat and poultry, customs, and immigration at the low end of that range; FDA, mine, and wage-hour compliance officers in the middle; and aviation inspectors at the top. Experienced environmental health inspectors at state levels earn $12,700 to $16,800 while their supervisors earn $18,200 to $24,300. Private industry pays $13,200 to $16,000 as a starting salary for inspectors with a B.A., experience brings them up to $18,000 to $22,000, and managers earn more than $25,000.

MEAT CUTTERS (BUTCHERS)

Did you know that the average American eats more than 175 pounds of meat a year? As a nation, we consume more than 35 billion pounds of beef, veal, pork, and lamb every twelve months. Your butcher is the link to the meat industry that makes all those roasts and chops and ribs available, not to mention chicken, game, and fish.

Not only do butchers have to know their cuts of meat, but they also have to know how to cut it, select it, care for it, and cure it. That means getting up at 4:00 A.M. and going to the wholesale meat markets (in large cities). It also means spending several hours a day working in a refrigerated room that is kept between 32 and 38 degrees Fahrenheit all year round. Most of the 204,000 meat cutters work for retail stores while others work for restaurants, hotels, and other institutions. An increasing number are employed at central cutting houses that prepare meat for several stores in one area.

The average wage for butchers employed by grocery stores is $8.32 an hour, making this one of the highest paid grocery store positions. Butchers who own their own shops or those who become involved in larger scale marketing earn more. This ancient trade is usually learned on the job although there are formal apprenticeship programs, in some cases affiliated with the union.

POLICE

Everyone is intrigued by the image of the policeman, from the five-year-old who wants to be one when he's grown up, to the adult who tries to avoid encounters with him.

Charged with maintaining public order, the police have a wide range of duties depending on the locale in which they work and the number of people on their force.

Local: There are only 450,000 local policemen and policewomen in this country, yet they are among the most frequently represented characters in the mythology of America—in stories, on television, and in films.

Some spend most of their days on the beat watching for possible trouble and answering emergency calls. Others direct traffic or keep crowds away from celebrities, or work as decoys in parks and shopping centers. A small number work in labs analyzing seized drugs or trying to match fingerprints.

Police are often called upon to work in extremely stressful situations. Candidates are carefully screened to see if they are physically and mentally capable of handling the pressures and dangers of the job. In most cases, applicants must be at least twenty-one years old and must fall within specified ranges of height and weight. Although a high school degree is not mandatory in all cases, the larger police departments do require it. While some cities accept law enforcement experience in lieu of academic training, there is increasing preference for candidates with a college background, particularly with work in sociology, psychology, and enforcement techniques. Police officers have further on-the-job training in constitutional law, civil rights, accident investigation, patrol, use of arms, defense, first aid, and specific emergency situations. Officers are encouraged to improve their abilities through advanced training, and departments often pay tuition for college courses.

Policemen and policewomen are promoted to the higher ranks of sergeant, lieutenant, and captain based on both performance and seniority. The starting salary ranges from $13,200 to $15,000 depending on the city in which they work, with increased experience bringing the annual earnings up to $16,550 to $18,000. Higher rank means higher salary. Sergeants earn from $16,000 to $18,000 while lieutenants start at $17,500. In emergencies, policemen must work overtime and obviously some work nights and weekends. Benefits are usually very good with liberal pension plans, possible early retirement, paid vacations and sick leave, and health coverage.

State: Throughout the United States there are about forty-seven thousand state police. California has the largest force with over five thousand. The smallest, North Dakota, has fewer than a hundred. Hawaii has none. In most of the states, applicants must have at least a high school education or equivalent and be at least twenty-one years old. In all of the states, recruits enter a formal training program and then serve a probationary period of six months to three years. Once the exclusive domain of men, state police forces are now taking on increasing numbers of women.

Although some of these "smokies" are needed for criminal investigation, the greatest demand is for work in highway patrol. In most states, state police are working forty-hour weeks and are covered by liberal pensions and other perks (i.e., medical and health insurance). Salaries begin at $13,200, while most state police average between $17,000 and $19,000 per year. Sergeants average between $15,450 and $19,300, and lieutenants average between $17,900 and $22,000.

PROGRAMMERS

There are approximately 247,000 programmers working with computers. They program computers with the information necessary to enable the computers to supply answers to complicated questions in a fraction of the time it would take a human being. Computers are useful and accurate only insofar as the information they are fed is precise and applicable. Our so-called electronic brains are quite stupid without the human intelligence that feeds them the data they require to answer our questions.

Programmers usually work from problems given to them by systems analysts. The problems can range from payroll deductions to the flight path of an orbiting satellite. In a sense, the programmer is the middleman. He gets information from analysts and is charged with feeding that information into the computer. The accuracy of his programming, of course, makes the computer brainy or brainless.

The weekly salary for trainee programmers is usually more than $240, and the job market is expanding. Talented programmers can earn in excess of $20,000 a year. However, competition looms with a number of independent companies providing complete software packages. New developments in computer techniques may also limit the need for future programmers.

16

Never spend your money
before you have it.
—JEFFERSON

EDUCATION

LIBRARIANS

With a liking for order, detail, information, and the literary arts, librarians manage the invaluable resources of mankind's accumulated knowledge. While the traditional image is of a bookish librarian chiefly interested in keeping readers silent, the job and the personnel have changed dramatically. Today's librarians perform a wide variety of tasks as they sort out and make accessible vast amounts of information. Many librarians specialize in a particular area such as children's books, audiovisual materials, extension services (bookmobiles), or a field of knowledge such as economics or law. Today a librarian not only leads you to catalogs and books, but he or she also works with film programs, storytelling hours, curriculum development, the programming of computerized information, and microfilm document storage.

Of the 142,000 professional librarians in this country, 40 percent work in schools, colleges, and universities, 20 percent in public libraries, and the rest in special libraries in companies, government agencies, and institutions.

Professional librarians are required to have a master's degree in library science. Candidates for a graduate program generally need four years of college, reading knowledge of one foreign language, and preferably a liberal arts background. Students in the graduate program specialize in their main area of interest. In many states, public school librarians must be certified both as teachers and as librarians.

A librarian's salary varies depending on background, experience, employer, and geographical location of the library. Recent graduates with an M.L.S. average $11,894, while college librarians earn an average of $16,930. The federal government pays beginners $14,097, but experienced federal librarians average $21,900. Jobs for librarians without additional skills are scarce, with half of today's graduates entering other occupations. However, related fields such as information-bank specialists are in demand.

LIBRARY TECHNICIANS

Library technicians assist librarians in both technical and user services that most libraries provide. Technical services involve research, keeping current files of new information in newspapers and periodicals, and tasks related to purchasing and cataloging new materials. User services involve greater interaction with the public in activities such as fact-finding, helping people use the catalogs, and participating in public or school programs that provide particular kinds of information.

There are more library technicians than librarians—172,000 in all. Most of them work in large school and public libraries, while about 3,600 work for the federal government in the Department of Defense and the Library of Congress. Training can be received on the job or in a formal program at a junior or community college. Some libraries do require the Associate of Arts degree in library technology that is the culmination of the formal two-year program. Credits earned in this course are also generally applicable toward a professional degree in library science.

This is a growing field for the eighties. With the expansion of services performed by libraries and the projected growth in school enrollment, there will be a greater need for technicians to assist librarians in all aspects of their work.

Library technicians working for the federal government average $12,100 a year. Most library workers also receive fringe benefits such as group insurance and retirement pay and, in some cases, educational assistance.

TEACHERS

Teachers teach in the hope that students will learn. It is possible that teachers pray a lot as well, because you can lead a boy to knowledge but you can't make him think.

Elementary school teachers usually act as surrogate parents in the early grades, where they teach basic concepts: the alphabet, arithmetic, art expression. Instruction gets more complex as the child matures: reading and writing skills, basic science, social organization, history. These teachers must have a bachelor's degree from an institution with an approved teacher education program. Their average earnings are about $14,669 per year. Salaries begin at $9,000 to $10,000.

High school teachers often act as mentors during the difficult period bridging adolescence and young adulthood. They are more specialized than most elementary school teachers in that they teach specific subjects. The subjects include English, algebra, biology, chemistry, social sciences, physics, and so on. The minimum requirement is a bachelor's degree and starting salaries are $9,500 to $11,000 depending on whether one goes into the field with a bachelor's or a master's degree. The average secondary school teacher in a public system earns $15,474.

College and university professors take over when, presumably, the traumas of "coming of age" have come and gone, with whatever shocks and scars they inevitably leave. There are usually four academic ranks at this level: instructor, assistant professor, associate professor, and full professor. Salaries go from about $12,500 for beginning instructors to $26,000 and more for full professors. Most positions require at least a master's degree, and full professors must have doctorates, extensive teaching experience, and a record of published books and articles. The average full-time faculty member earns about $22,000.

Competition for teaching jobs is expected to be sharp for the next five years, but because of population patterns, the demand for teachers is expected to increase. The best paid teaching jobs are in Alaska where the starting salary is more than $20,000 per year.

17

It is not a custom with me
to keep money to look at.
—WASHINGTON

SALES

BUYERS AND PURCHASING AGENTS

Caveat emptor is a Latin expression meaning, "let the buyer beware," an admonition that a buyer in a free market is free to make mistakes without recourse to recovering losses.

Buyers and purchasing agents acquire merchandise for their firms to resell. The merchandise can range anywhere from Givenchy frocks to manure spreaders. The frock buyer may make his purchases in Paris; the manure spreader buyer may make his purchases in South Bend, Indiana. But they both serve the same function. Whether they are dealing with the same product is a matter of opinion.

Buyers are given great latitude in their judgments. Those judgments have to be made quickly with a secure knowledge of what the market will pay for the product the buyer purchases. Obviously, the best buyers are those who pay the least for merchandise that sells for the most, whatever the nature of the goods. Buyers earn between $23,000 and $32,000 a year, but some earn a great deal more.

Purchasing agents also buy goods for their firms, but the goods they buy are used by the firms themselves. Purchasing agents are concerned with inventories. They buy replacement equipment at the best possible prices in order to keep the firm's operations uninterrupted. The starting salary for junior purchasing agents is about $13,000, while experienced ones may average $16,200, and senior agents in technical lines may make $19,600 on the average. The average salary in the federal government is $22,239. Because the knowledge required to do their jobs effectively is very specialized, buyers and purchasing agents are among the highest paid jobs in industry. No formal educational requirements are stipulated. The knowledge may be acquired on the job or through study, but the work or educational background of the individual is obviously important in setting the salary range.

More than 250,000 people are working in these fields and their salaries may go up to and beyond $50,000 a year for managing a large department. The field is notorious for kickbacks and payoffs, since marketing decisions can make or break suppliers and vendors.

CREDIT MANAGERS

Santa Claus or Scrooge? If you enjoy being in a position to grant or deny large sums of money, the life of a credit manager may be for you. People and businesses needing additional money turn over their financial records to a credit manager and hope for the best. The credit manager then makes a judgment for or against the loan, based on the personal interview, bank statements, previous loan history, and reports from credit agencies. A credit manager is like the watchdog of a giant estate: eager for red meat but wary of biting the wrong party.

As the guardian of a great treasure, a credit manager making $30,000 a year can say "no" to a president of a company who makes $200,000 a year, about a loan of $1 million. Money makes money as long as the credit manager is sensitive to the ebbs and flows of the business cycle. If people and companies cannot or will not pay back their loans, the financial institution will go under.

Ordinarily, a college degree is needed for this job, although some high school graduates with experience in debt collecting or processing information may be considered. Trainees begin by analyzing past transactions to learn the signs that distinguish a bad credit risk.

Working a nine-to-five day, a credit manager may oversee an office staff as they gather and process information, contact a customer who is not making payments on time, interview a new applicant, and give final approval to another. For his efforts, he is paid a middle manager's salary, between $20,000 and $30,000. Top credit managers sometimes earn as much as $40,000—a far cry from the starting salary of $13,000 for assistants.

FASHION MODELS

There are a million broken arches for every klieg light on Seventh Avenue. For fashion models, New York's garment district is mecca. But the game is tough, and the heels are as high as the stakes.

Most models show clothes to live audiences. In the chic salons of New York haute couture, this may mean acting, dancing, swinging down the runway to music, and full stage effects. In most showrooms it may be enough to walk straight and do a neat turn.

Not all jobs are in New York. There are modeling jobs in department stores from Toledo to Sheboygan. And both Chicago and Los Angeles have their own smaller fashion industries. There are also other kinds of modeling jobs in New York. Fitting models may type and file for much of the year, then try on and display the new line of coats in the spring and fall. Photographic models pose by the assignment for still photographers who, in turn, work for advertising agencies or magazines. Some models work exclusively in film and television commercials.

Most fashion models are female, but some are male. How they are paid, and how much, depends on the nature of the work. The very best fashion models working full-time for manufacturers or wholesalers earn salaries of more than $35,000 a year. Those who do retail shows are paid by the job and must work a great deal to equal that annual salary. They also pay an agent (who books them) a percentage of their hourly rate, which averages between $75 and $100 for women and up to $75 for male models. Television commercials pay union scale: approximately $145 for an extra; $200 and up for a principal, plus residuals when the commercial is rerun.

In modeling, looks are everything. Female fashion models must be between 5 feet 7 inches and 5 feet 9½ inches and weigh between 110 and 122 pounds. Males must be at least 6 feet tall and wear a size 40 suit. Photographic models must be thinner than fashion models because the camera adds 10 pounds to one's appearance. They must also have fine regular features, wide-set eyes, a long neck, good teeth, hands, and legs.

Modeling schools are one way to learn style, makeup, and some of the tricks of the trade, but they do not secure employment for their graduates. Other kinds of training, such as dancing, art, drama, and fashion design, can be equally good preparation for modeling, and may later provide a secondary career, a useful asset since models stop working as soon as their youth, or their style, begins to fade.

GASOLINE SERVICE STATION ATTENDANTS

Pumping gas used to be the first job a teenager had. It still is, but local service stations no longer need as many employees because of the rise in gas prices and self-service pumps. Unless there's a long gas line, gasoline attendants are usually gratefully appreciated by the drivers whose cars they refuel and service. In addition to pumping gas, service station attendants provide routine checks of oil, water, air pressure in the tires, and so on. In some cases attendants also sell and install small parts such as batteries and headlights, while other employees who specialize in mechanics do the more complicated repairs.

Service station attendants receive their training on the job. More than one-third work part-time, often with schedules that include evenings, weekends, and holidays. Wages range from $2.50 to $4.00 an hour, while many attendants also earn commissions based on the value of the products they sell. Possibilities for advancement include positions as automobile mechanics, station managers, and sales representatives for oil companies. Because of the large number of people employed in this work (340,000) and the relatively high turnover rate, there are many openings each year.

REAL ESTATE AGENTS AND BROKERS

Real estate brokers, and the agents who work for them, represent property owners who wish to sell or rent their properties. Brokers and their agents bring together a seller or lessor and a "willing, ready, and able" buyer or lessee and get a commission for doing so. Commission rates for home brokerage vary and are negotiable, but the national average is 6 percent. They also draw up contracts and make arrangements for mortgages and other types of financing, while trying to keep a pleasant face when Mrs. Jones says: "Wouldn't it be nice if the third floor were on the first floor and the first floor were on the second floor?"

Today agents must be trained and pass state examinations. Brokers have to take extended courses and pass more stringent examinations. This is a highly competitive field and persons who genuinely enjoy selling can find an occupation in what is deemed to be a growing job opportunity market. Agents have been earning about $16,500 a year, and the brokers who employ them have been earning twice that amount, $33,000. Agents are frequently involved in finding "listings," which results in splitting commissions between the agent who finds the seller and the agent who finds the buyer.

Virtually all brokers own their own businesses. Agents must serve an apprenticeship, usually two years, before they can qualify for the broker's examination.

STOCKBROKERS

"Bulls make money, bears make money, but pigs get slaughtered" is an old Wall Street saying. The expert who protects investors from being too greedy is the securities salesperson; he/she advises when to sell and when to buy shares of a company (representing fractional ownership) or its bonds (representing debt of the company).

There are over forty thousand publicly owned companies whose securities are widely traded. The intermediaries between buyers and sellers are thirty-six thousand stockbrokers, registered representatives who work for member firms of the leading stock exchanges, such as the New York and American exchanges, or for over-the-counter brokerage houses that are members of the National Association of Securities Dealers. Prospective brokers must pass an examination on the securities business, for which training courses are given at the larger brokerage houses or at specialized business schools.

A knowledgeable broker, one who follows the economic trends of the nation, financial trends of various industries, and the business fortunes of some special companies, may make a good deal of money for his/her clients by astute trading and timely transactions. A broker may also make a decent salary, plus significant commission; usually 33 percent of the commission is rebated to him/her by the brokerage house.

Prospects for the business vary directly with the health of the economy. In periods of recession, the brokerage business is not a growth industry. However, stockbrokers have in recent years expanded their financial services (such as selling financial planning, tax shelters, and insurance) so that they are not so dependent on stock market activity. While some brokers make less than $30,000 a year, most make more: $100,000 a year is not uncommon if a broker has a loyal and active following, plus a few institutional clients who transact their business with him.

UNDERWRITERS

Insurance companies insure people against losses: loss of life, property, money, almost anything. Betty Grable's legs were said to have been insured for one million dollars; whether that policy meant loss of legs or included the development of fat ankles is not known. The likelihood is the policy was a press agent's fancy.

Underwriters tell insurance companies whether a risk is a good risk. They specialize in estimating the probability of loss by examining information on insurance applications, reports from loss-control consultants, medical reports, and other study sources.

There are no specific requirements for entering the field, but insurance companies tend to seek college graduates who have majored in business administration or liberal arts. Starting salaries average about $14,000 a year. Experienced underwriters get about $18,600. Supervisors can get as much as $25,000 annually.

18

It is hard for an empty sack
to stand upright.
—BENJAMIN FRANKLIN

CONSTRUCTION

BRICKLAYERS

Just for the record, a bricklayer lays bricks and a hod carrier carries them, along with a hod, which is the tray on which the mortar is put after it has been mixed. Bricklaying is one ancient trade that shows no sign of dying away, and so far there seems to be no satisfactory way to mechanize it. Some people lay bricks for relaxation. Indeed, Winston Churchill, among his other talents, was a card-carrying bricklayer.

There are about 204,000 bricklayers, stonemasons, and marble setters. Newcomers learn the trade through apprenticeships set up by local union-management committees. The usual program is three years of on-the-job training and 144 hours of classroom instruction in blueprint reading and the like. Applicants must be seventeen or older. The total hours a bricklayer puts in can be limited by rain, snow, or a recession. Consequently, hourly wages are high: marble setters average $10.75 per hour; bricklayers, $11.05; stonemasons, $11.25.

BULLDOZER OPERATOR/HEAVY EQUIPMENT OPERATOR

Lifting that bale is easier now that we have giant cranes—and pushing it around is a piece of cake, given the bulldozer.

There really isn't much to running a bulldozer; it's a lot like driving a car. The blade at the front is raised and lowered by push button or lever, and the rest is pretty much a question of patience, as well as forward and reverse. The crane is another story. It takes nerve and accurate judgment of distances and heights to push and pull a series of buttons, pedals, and levers in split-second sequence to ensure the proper placement of a quarter-ton pane of glass in an 8-by-10-foot window opening, ten stories above the ground.

There are about 580,000 heavy equipment operating engineers: 120,000 are bulldozer operators; the rest operate cranes, derricks, hoists, air compressors, trench-pipe layers, and dredges. Most are employed by private contractors in highway, dam, airport, and other large-scale projects. Others work for utility or manufacturing companies. Jobs are spread throughout the country, including some very remote locations.

A three-year formal apprenticeship program is the best way to become an operating engineer. These programs are generally sponsored by a local union-management committee, but are also available in the armed forces. Job opportunities should be fairly plentiful in the decades to come. Spring and summer are the best times to look, since this field is closely tied to the construction cycle. Operators of heavy machinery can expect to earn between $9.50 and $10.50 per hour.

CONSTRUCTION WORKERS

Working on construction is one way to receive a high hourly wage while learning skills that can lead to craftsman jobs such as bricklayer or cement mason. You have to be in very good physical shape, of course.

Construction workers do all kinds of work, from tearing down old buildings and filling concrete mixers to blasting rock and using laser beam equipment in the construction of tunnels. Generally, no formal training is required to get a job as a construction laborer, but beginners are assigned the simpler tasks until they learn how to lay large pipes, or pave a highway, or how to drill different kinds of rock. In addition to learning on the job, contractors and unions have set up one-to-two-month training programs for employees to teach the use of certain machines and safety measures for work that is more complex.

There are 860,000 construction workers in the United States. Many have transferred from other nonsupervisory jobs that do not pay nearly as well. However, all construction work, whether erecting new buildings or digging ditches, is subject to weather and economic conditions, so the annual earnings may not be as high as the hourly rate would indicate. On average, construction workers are paid $8.50 per hour.

ELECTRICIANS

Most people are content to let electricians handle the live wires, which means plenty of work and very little kibitzing from the client. This is one of the best paid construction trades: the hourly rate is over $12, plus guaranteed overtime and fringe benefits. It is also relatively steady work, since electricians can switch to factory, maintenance, or shipbuilding when housing construction slows down.

One way (though not the most frequent) to become a construction electrician is by first mastering the maintenance trade. Still, it's one thing to fix wiring and another to install it. First, conduit or tubing is run through the building inside the walls, with metal switches fastened on the walls. Then insulated wire is pulled through the tubes and fastened to the outlets to complete the circuit. (Then you turn on the main electrical supply and see what lights up.)

Most of the 270,000 construction electricians work for electrical contractors, but many are self-employed. Jobs are concentrated in urban areas and should increase faster than average during the 1980s.

Aspiring electricians should be agile, careful vocational or high school graduates who are not color-blind (wiring is color-coded). A formal apprenticeship is the best way to start, indeed the only way in some cities where unions are especially powerful.

GLAZIERS

Responsible for cutting glass and installing it in windows, doors, and walls of buildings, glaziers use refined skills to work with a delicate medium. Most of the nineteen thousand glaziers work for contractors in a trade that is closely tied into the construction industry. Most of them, too, work in urban areas.

The average wage for a union construction glazier in a metropolitan area is $10.40 an hour. However, this relatively high hourly rate is balanced by the fact that the annual number of hours worked can be adversely affected by bad weather or slow building periods.

Glaziers usually learn their trade through a four-year apprentice program sponsored by local union-management committees. In addition to on-the-job training, the program includes classroom instruction in mathematics, blueprint reading, general construction techniques, and safety practices. The demand for glaziers is expected to increase with the ongoing demand for new residential and commercial buildings, especially those with lots of windows.

INSULATION WORKERS

This is one of the most rapidly growing specializations of the eighties thanks to the astronomic price of fuel oil. Insulation of homes and commercial buildings as well as insulation of heating and cooling equipment plays an essential part in the effort to conserve energy. Insulation specialists select the most appropriate type of insulation for each situation and then follow through by installing it.

Insulation workers are most often employed by contractors or by large plants and factories that have extensive piping systems requiring maintenance and repair. Most of the fifty-one thousand insulation workers have learned this art on the job or in a four-year training program called an improvership. As in most other building trades, the four-year training program provides a broader background so that the person who completes it will be able to do varied kinds of work in the field.

Insulation specialists tend to work in urban areas and their union wages there average $10.90 an hour. Apprentices start at about half that rate. Nonunion insulation workers earn between $220 and $325 a week.

IRONWORKERS

Ironworkers are responsible for erecting the structural framework for the metal buildings of today and tomorrow. Without a support structure, no building would be able to reach into the sky. Following blueprints, as do so many workers in the construction industry, ironworkers place steel parts in concrete foundations, fasten the steel framework of bridges, set up and rig heavy hoisting equipment, and install metal stairways, catwalks, and window frames. Often ironworkers must walk and work on narrow steel girders high above the ground. Obviously, they do not suffer from acrophobia and are physically strong.

There are more than seventy-eight thousand ironworkers and the field is expected to continue to grow through the mid-1980s, following continuing growth in construction. Training is recommended through an apprenticeship program usually sponsored by union-contractor agreements; the program combines classroom work in drafting and mathematics with on-the-job learning. Average wages are $10.85 an hour, with apprentices starting at 60 percent of that rate. Again, as in other construction-related fields, work is often limited by weather so that annual earnings may not be as high as the hourly rate indicates.

LATHERS

Working in the construction industry, lathers install wire mesh or gypsum sheets to which cement and plaster adhere. The various kinds of metal and gypsum supports are called lath, and without them a cement wall or ceiling would just fall down. Lathers install suspended ceilings, they build frames to fit on ornamental or curved shapes, and they make the lath backing for theatrical scenery.

Most of the twenty-three thousand lathers in the United States belong to the Wood, Wire, and Metal Lathers International Union. Their union wages average $10.05 an hour but, again, since they sometimes cannot work in bad weather, their yearly salary is not as high as it may seem.

Lathers learn their trade as apprentices to an experienced worker or in programs set up by labor-management committees. In the formal program there are classroom lessons in mathematics, blueprint reading, sketching, estimating, basic welding, and safety.

ROOFERS

Roofers are building construction specialists whose expertise is in making roofs watertight. They also frequently waterproof walls and floors.

Historically, they have been experts at applying asphalt, felt, shingles, tiles, and slate to roof surfaces; however, the introduction of new materials in recent years has simplified their once tedious task. In a few years the ever-present kettle of hot tar will probably vanish from their inventory as rubber and plastic composition rolls replace the traditional tar paper.

Some 114,000 roofers have been employed in the United States in recent years and their number is expected to increase at a rate greater than the general average. A three-year apprenticeship program is normally required, as well as about 144 hours of classroom instruction in a construction trade school where the emphasis is on things like blueprint reading and the mathematics of square-foot measurement.

Union roofers in metropolitan areas have been averaging about $9.60 an hour, almost twice that of production workers in other private industries. But it must be remembered that employment is seasonal. Little roofing is done during the winter months. The work is often strenuous and sometimes hazardous because of the risk of slips and falls. If you're afraid of heights, don't try to climb to this occupation.

SHEET METAL WORKERS

Sheet metal is exactly what it sounds like: metal spread out in thin sheets. Sheet metal workers fabricate and install sheet metal products such as ducts for air-conditioning, heating, and ventilating systems, flat metal for kitchen walls and counters, stamped metal for roofing and siding. Working from blueprint specifications, sheet metal workers measure, cut, bend, and shape the metal into ducts, pipes, tubes, elbows, and other items to conduct the flow of air or secure surfaces against air or liquid leakage.

Employment opportunities for sheet metal workers fluctuate with the expansion or the contraction of the construction industry. For the most part, sheet metal workers get their training on the job during a four-year period, which is usually accompanied by classroom instruction. Demand for sheet metal workers is expected to increase at the same rate as the average for all occupations through the mid-1980s.

Union sheet metal workers in urban areas have been averaging more than $10 per hour, about twice the average for all production, nonsupervisory workers in private industry. Apprentices start out at about 45 percent of the skilled workers' average.

WELDERS

While some welders fasten the metal joints of the sculptures of Calder, Nevelson, and Noguchi, others fasten the steel plates in ships or repair the beams of bridges or seal the cores of nuclear reactors. All of them are masked, wearing protective helmets, goggles, clothing, and shoes as they work with metals at high intensities of heat.

There are a variety of welding processes requiring different types and levels of skill. The most common manual method is arc welding: an electrical current is set up between a welding rod and the materials to be joined, and the heat of the current melts the metals. Gas welding uses tanks of fuel such as acetylene or hydrogen and a torch as well as a rod of metal filler. In both of the above methods, the welder must know exactly how much heat is needed and where it has to be applied for each particular joint. Another kind of welding that requires fewer decisions is used in industries that mass-produce metal parts. In automotive factories, for example, welding equipment is manipulated by operators but it automatically supplies the proper amount of heat and metal filler. Even more highly automated machines are used when there are numerous identical parts to be welded and the operator simply positions the parts and pushes a button.

One-third of the 679,000 welders and flame cutters (who cut metal with the same tools welders use to join it) work in Pennsylvania, Ohio, Michigan, Indiana, and Illinois. Two-thirds work in the production of heavy equipment such as trucks, boilers, machinery, and ships, while others work in construction and bridge and pipe repair.

A skilled welder needs several years of training to learn his craft. Beginners learning on the job may work on simple welding processes where one metal part is being welded repeatedly. Some companies train employees as welders; there are also apprenticeship programs that take several years to complete.

Welders who work on crucial joints are often required to pass a welding exam and become certified welders.

Welders working with automated equipment earn between $6 and $7 per hour, while those in construction earn between $9 and $12. Most welders belong to a union, the particular one depending upon the field in which they work.

19

> Capitalists are no more capable of self-sacrifice than a man is capable of lifting himself by his own bootstraps.
>
> —LENIN

TRANSPORTATION

AIRPLANE PILOTS

It takes fifteen hundred hours of experience—including jet flying time—to get an airline transport pilot's license. Then you can be hired by any airline and, after fifteen to twenty years of accumulated seniority, it's possible to become the captain of a commercial airliner. Even if you join the air force and use their jets to tote up your flying hours, this is one of the heaviest personal investments required for any career. It pays off, for the few who make it, at more than $80,000 to $110,000 a year.

No doubt the airlines' superb safety record is the result of the care with which pilots are selected, trained, and tested. Besides being subjected to yearly testing on aircraft as well as written exams, candidates for hiring by commercial airlines undergo intensive psychological scrutiny and physical examinations to determine their ability to make quick, judicious decisions under pressure and to work with other crew members. Those who pass muster then begin the long internship: five to ten years as a flight engineer (starting at $14,400 a year); then ten to twenty years as copilot ($12,000 to $60,000) before finally making captain. Changing to another airline means starting over, so hiring is usually a lifetime career commitment.

Of eighty-three thousand civilian pilots, only about half work for the airlines. Other pilots fly cargo or executive passenger planes, air taxis, sight-seeing or crop-dusting planes. Still others work as flight instructors or inspectors, often at the same time accumulating their flying hours to qualify as airline pilots. Both pay and perquisites are less attractive for the business pilot. Although the captain of a company jet may make up to $60,000 a year, he is likely to be responsible for maintenance, record keeping, and supervision of baggage loading and fueling, so he has less free time between flights. All pilots have irregular schedules and most can count on spending a fair amount of time away from home.

There are still only a few female pilots and relatively few minority fliers. This is unlikely to change, since the short-term job outlook is poor and many new jobs that are created will be filled by pilots presently on furlough. Competition will be keen, even for well-trained college graduates, and the cost of acquiring flying experience will make military training the only feasible route for many aspiring pilots. The Airline Pilots' Association recommends that all pilots have second careers to tide them over possible furloughs of one to seven years at various stages in their careers. Indeed, many return to the air force in slack times.

AIR TRAFFIC CONTROLLERS

As an airplane crosses the skies, it passes over successive teams of two or three air traffic controllers who radio up the latest weather reports and positions of nearby planes. Larger teams in control towers at airports direct smooth takeoffs, landings, and holding patterns. This job takes steady nerves, clear speech, and the ability to make rapid decisions. The Federal Aviation Administration (FAA) is a cautious and benevolent employer, as well as the only one for civilians.

In order to take the Federal Civil Service System Test, an applicant must be under thirty-one, in excellent health with vision correctable to 20/20, and have three years of work experience, four years of college, or a combination of both. After they pass the initial test and complete a sixteen-week training period at the FAA Academy in Oklahoma City and the two or three years of experience required to become fully qualified, controllers still must pass one physical and two job performance exams every year. That is the cautious part. However, a new recruit can look forward to a liberal retirement program, thirteen to twenty-six days of paid vacation every year, thirteen sick days, reduced air fares, good possibilities for transfer, and advancement into higher echelons in the FAA.

Controllers start work earning $12,500 a year. The future will find more jobs there, and a number of qualified applicants will be ready to fill them. Air traffic controllers work a forty-hour week, including nights and weekends on a rotating schedule to keep the vigil constant. For their efforts, air traffic controllers can expect to work their way up to an average salary of $25,400.

BUS DRIVERS (LOCAL AND INTER-CITY)

The market for bus drivers, local and inter-city, is expected to expand more than any other driving occupation except trucking during the 1980s. The pay is good and, for those who do not intend to go to college, this is a career with a number of attractions: there is a strong union that guarantees a good salary, and one can be assured of full job benefits. Of course, it isn't quite like driving a car; trainees can expect to spend several weeks learning defensive driving techniques as well as behind-the-wheel maneuvers and must take a stiff written test before they are allowed even a practice run with an experienced driver. Then they may remain on the "extra" list, working replacement shifts for over a year before being assigned a regular route. Drivers with top seniority can choose the runs they prefer, avoiding overtime and heavy traffic.

There are about eighty-one thousand local bus drivers employed, and about twenty-five thousand others drive between cities. While similar skills are required for both types of jobs, there is a difference in the nature of the driving: long stretches of highway versus stopping and starting in city traffic or winding through suburban streets. Also, inter-city drivers are paid more than local drivers, earning average salaries in excess of $16,000.

CABDRIVERS

The opportunity to perform for a continually changing captive audience is not to be taken lightly. This may account for the high percentage of aspiring actors driving cabs—and practicing monologues. (Those who "make it" can go on to become dispatchers, and monopolize the two-way radio.)

Of course, some people just like to drive. Whether they work for a fleet company or own and operate their own taxis, cabdrivers are very much in control of their cruising locations and, therefore, of their own income. (Even those who work for a company either rent their cabs and keep the take, or work on a commission basis.) And cabdrivers' manners and efficiency affect their tips, which amount to 10 to 20 percent of the fare.

There are ninety-four thousand full-time taxi drivers, one-fifth of them in New York City. There are a few jobs in small towns, but the bulk of the business is in metropolitan areas. Although this is a shrinking rather than a growing job market, there will still be many jobs throughout the 1980s due to rapid turnover within the field.

There is great variation in the way cabdrivers are employed and in local licensing requirements. A national average rate of about $3.90 per hour, including tips, was reported in one private survey. Union contracts indicate that company drivers are usually guaranteed a $14.00 to $18.50 minimum per day. It is best to check with local cab companies on everything from licensing procedures to job and wage prospects in the area.

CONDUCTORS

We all probably know more about the romance of the railroads than the reality—the huffing and puffing of the Little Engine That Could, Woody Guthrie hopping freight trains, the mighty rushing engine of the Wabash Cannonball. What part do conductors play in these ceaseless transnational journeys? More than taking tickets, that's for sure.

Conductors supervise both the train and yard crews and are responsible for the train getting to its destination on time. On the train the conductors maintain close contact by radio with dispatchers, brake operators, and engineeers. They monitor the condition of the cars and rails, and if it's necessary for the train to stop or switch tracks, they alert the engineer.

Conductors working in train yards direct the assembling and moving of trains, making sure that the caboose isn't coupled to the engine. In modernized yards they use electronic equipment to switch cars to the appropriate tracks.

All of the 34,200 conductors have had to move up the ranks. At first they work as extras filling in as conductors when needed but otherwise working as brake operators. Scheduling and promotions are based on seniority with the possibility of advancing to trainmaster or yardmaster.

Yard conductors work a regular forty-hour week while road conductors are called to travel at all hours of the day and night. The latter are paid by the number of miles traveled or hours worked, whichever is greater. The average monthly salary for a yard conductor is $1,815; a passenger train conductor earns $2,188 and a freight conductor $2,290.

FLIGHT ATTENDANTS

The average passenger on an airline flight is a bit apprehensive, no matter how many miles he or she has flown; an important part of the flight attendant's job is to put the passenger at ease. To do so requires poise, tact, conversational ability, and a good degree of physical stamina.

Flight attendants, also called stewardesses and stewards, are paid to make the passengers' flights safe, comfortable, and enjoyable. Attendants check tickets, serve beverages and meals, ensure that seat belts are fastened, assist elderly and handicapped persons, and help care for small children. Attendants must also be prepared to assist in evacuating planes in the event of an emergency landing and to administer first aid when required.

Generally, applicants must be nineteen years old, high school graduates, and in excellent health. Those who have spent time in nurses' training, college, or dealing with the public are given preference.

The monthly earnings of all flight attendants average more than $1,200. Job opportunities are expected to grow at a much faster rate than average during the next five years as flight travel continues to expand. Travel discounts for attendants and their immediate families are additional inducements.

MERCHANT MARINE OFFICERS AND SAILORS

There are 38,300 seamen, of which 13,500 are officers, employed aboard United States oceangoing vessels. Applicants for an officer's license in the deck or engineering departments must be at least twenty-one, and meet certain legal and medical requirements. Candidates must also have at least three years of appropriate sea experience or be a graduate of an approved training program.

The captain or master of an oceangoing ship is the lawful

representative of the shipowner. He is charged with total responsibility for the operation and safety of the vessel, and the health and welfare of crew, passengers, and cargo. For this weighty charge, merchant captains are paid an average $4,159 per month. The first mate is the captain's chief assistant, assigning duties and overseeing operations, maintenance, and discipline. First mates, or chief mates as they are sometimes called, earn an average $2,259 per month. The officer in charge of engines, power plant, and related works is the chief engineer. Marine engineers are highly prized and their base pay is second only to the ship's captain: chief engineers earn an average $3,779. Radio officers earn an average $1,920 per month, and the officer in charge of paperwork and money, the purser, is compensated least of all the ship's officers, with an average base pay of $1,217.

Of course it takes more than officers to run a merchant vessel. The highest paid seamen are electricians, earning an average $1,337 per month. The man responsible for the victuals, the chief steward, makes $1,136 per month, while the one responsible for preparing them, the cook, earns $984 per month. At the bottom of the rung are the able seamen with base pay rates of $865 per month and ordinary seamen with pay of $675 per month. Monthly wages for both officers and seamen are supplemented by premium pay for overtime and other factors. On the average, premium earnings are equal to 50 percent of base wages.

At the end of World War II this country possessed the largest merchant marine ever assembled. It has gone downhill since. Because it costs twice as much to operate a ship with American crews due to high wages, more and more ships are being registered abroad. Few new ships are being built and those that are require fewer crew members. In the national interest, the federal government is committed to subsidizing new ship construction, thus ensuring future jobs. However, laborsaving automation will limit the number of new jobs provided, and the employment outlook is expected to decline.

TRAVEL AGENTS

Not too long ago only the rich could afford to travel. Now virtually everyone travels. Travel agents are in the business of making arrangements for travelers, that is, making the best possible reservations on planes, boats, at hotels, even restaurants and theaters, taking into consideration the tastes and budgets of those who come to them for service.

There are roughly six thousand travel agencies in the United States, employing about 18,500 agents. Agency owners depend on commissions from airlines and other carriers, tour operators, and places of lodging for their income. The commissions vary from 5 to 10 percent. Salaries of hired agents vary from $10,000 to $15,000. An individual agency owner can, obviously, make as much as his bookings allow.

Travel agents almost always travel at reduced rates throughout the world. And so they travel a great deal. The field is expanding, but the competition is expected to be stiff in the next five years. It seems a good many people want to get away from it all, including travel agents.

20

Money is like a sixth sense
—and you can't make use
of the other five without it.
—W. SOMERSET MAUGHAM

SCIENTIFIC AND TECHNICAL

ASTRONOMERS AND ASTROPHYSICISTS

Astronomers and astrophysicists are usually also teachers. They analyze data gleaned from observatory research and present their findings hoping they have come closer to the fundamental patterns that are the nature of the universe. The tools available to them are fabulously expensive and fun to use—spectroscopes, radio telescopes, computers to work out mathematical equations. Nevertheless, many astronomers work only in the theoretical realm and rarely use the actual observatories.

Slightly under one-third of all working astronomers are federal employees of the National Aeronautical and Space Administration and the Department of Defense. A bachelor's or master's degree in astronomy can get you a job as an assistant in a planetarium or as a research assistant. Ph.D.'s qualify to teach in colleges and to do research of their own. Some teach math and physics as well.

Very few people work in this field—only two thousand or so last year, and the job openings are expected to remain scarce. Starting astronomers earn between $20,000 and $23,500, but federal employees average in excess of $33,000. A few astronomical superstars, such as Carl Sagan and Robert Jastrow, earn free trips on the *Queen Elizabeth II* and spots on "The Merv Griffin Show."

BIOCHEMISTS

Ever since the romance of the atom yielded to the glamour of the gene in the late 1960s, biochemists have commanded a major share of media attention and federal research dollars. There are twenty thousand biochemists in the United States. More than three out of four do basic research, studying the complex chemical combinations that are the basis of life and control reproduction, growth, and heredity. Applied researchers in biochemistry use the results of this basic research to solve practical problems in agriculture, medicine, or nutrition.

Half of all biochemists are employed in the research labs and classrooms of universities. Another 25 percent work in private industry, with the remainder employed in nonprofit research institutes and government agencies. A Ph.D. degree is vital for any significant research or administrative role, but a bachelor's degree in biochemistry is sufficient to enter the field as a lab technician or research assistant.

Biochemists are well paid, averaging about twice the annual salary for all nonsupervisory workers except farmers. Experienced biochemists with Ph.D. degrees make about $28,000 per year. The need to find cures for cancer and other major diseases, and public concern with environmental protection, should keep the government money rolling in, resulting in a steady growth in the number of jobs.

BIOLOGISTS

Biology is the study of living things, so a biologist may well have the forest or field or zoo as a laboratory. Of course, the image of the white-coated scientist at the centrifuge is also realistic. Biology labs, whether they are located in university research centers, hospitals, or private drug companies, are generally clean, well-lighted places, and working conditions are pleasant, although the work itself may be more painstaking and repetitive than the movies make it seem.

A knowledge of computers and of technical equipment like the electron microscope is essential for the technician who will operate them, as well as for the advanced research biologist who analyzes the results. And it goes without saying that a complete grounding in general biology and an advanced degree in a specialty are required. A Ph.D. is necessary for most college teaching jobs, independent research, and administrative work. A master's degree is sufficient for many jobs in applied research.

Biologists are well paid, with an average annual salary of $23,800 if they are employed by the federal government. Ph.D.'s could begin at that level and advance well beyond it. In private industry, bioengineering is one of the most exciting areas: it is also the field that commands salaries in excess of $50,000 for work in recombinant DNA technology.

The more traditional subdisciplines of biology involve the study of specific organisms. Botanists deal with plants, identifying and classifying them, or work on cures for plant diseases. Agronomists are concerned with plants on the larger scale, working to improve the quality and yield of crops, or erosion control. Horticulturists develop superior strains of orchard or garden plants, and beautify parks and community spaces. Some biologists are zoologists; zoologists can be ornithologists (studying birds) or entomologists (studying insects) or mammalogists (studying mammals), and so on.

Other fields of biology are defined by a type of activity rather than by a type of living thing: ecologists are interested in the relationship of all sorts of plants and animals to their environment; microbiologists study anything small enough to require a microscope to see it such as bacteria, viruses, and molds; nutritionists study the way in which the body utilizes food; pathologists specialize in the effects of diseases, parasites, and insects on human cells.

Although employment opportunities for biologists with advanced degrees are expected to be good through the mid-1980s, competition will be tougher for jobs at a lower level. However, overall employment growth will be sustained in biology and related fields due to increased interest in the natural environment and in medical research.

CHEMISTS

Far from the standard image of the eccentric old doctor hovering over a simmering flask that is about to explode, the real chemist of today is usually found working calmly and meticulously in a clean, well-appointed lab. The test tubes and microscopes he or she uses are employed in basically nonhazardous experiments to determine the composition of moon rocks, to create a more efficient jet fuel, or to perfect the wrinkle-free sheet. Rather than causing it, the chemist may be working to eliminate chemical pollution, and to purify as well as preserve food products.

Chemists search for and put into practical use new knowledge about substances. Analytical chemists (like those who analyzed the moon rocks) examine the basic structure, composition, and nature of substances. Organic chemists specialize in the study of all carbon compounds, from people to plastics. Inorganic chemists work with what's left, the noncarbon compounds that, for example, may be used in solid-state electronic components. Physical chemists study energy transformations, and biochemists study the chemistry of life, both of which are burgeoning fields for the near future.

About three-fifths of the 140,000 chemists employed work in private industry, and this number is expected to grow substantially in the 1980s. Product development will continue to be the major thrust of applied chemistry, but there will also be growth in the field due to the need to solve energy shortages, to perfect environmental control, and to contribute to better health care.

Half of all the chemists work in six states: New York, New Jersey, California, Pennsylvania, Ohio, and Illinois. Nearly 20 percent of them work in just four cities: New York, Chicago, Philadelphia, and Newark.

As expected, average salaries vary according to the experience and education of the individual scientist. An experienced chemist with a bachelor's degree averages $23,900 a year; with a master's, $25,400, and with a Ph.D., $29,200. Starting salaries in private industry are about the same as those in government. Relatively few chemists are teaching and doing research in colleges and universities. They tend to earn less than their colleagues in private industry, but generally are able to supplement their salaries with income from consulting and writing. Competition for university spots will be keen in the coming decade, since little growth is anticipated in this area of employment.

ENGINEERS

Engineers are the human bridges between scientific theory and practical application. From abstract concepts they design machinery, products, systems, and processes for industrial and manufacturing use. Engineers constitute the second largest professional group in the country, behind teachers.

There are more than twenty-five recognized engineering specialties, with electrical engineers as the largest branch of the engineering profession. They design, develop, test, supervise, and maintain electrical and electronic equipment. Industrial engineers are more concerned with business systems than other engineers. They are charged with solving organizational, production, and related problems dealing with manpower, machines, and materials, trying to find the most efficient and least costly method of creating a given product or service. Mechanical engineers are occupied with devising the most economical production, transmission, and use of power. They design and supervise the development of power-producing machines such as internal-combustion engines, steam and gas turbines, and jet and rocket engines. Metallurgical engineers develop methods to process metals for conversion into useful products. They are sought by the metalworking industries in order to develop new metal alloys, as well as to devise new uses for existing metals. Mining engineers locate minerals and supervise their mining and preparation so that various manufacturing industries can utilize them. These engineers are responsible for the layouts of open pits and underground mine shafts and tunnels, as well as the development of transportation systems to get these minerals to the factories that will use them.

More than half of all engineers work in manufacturing industries, and virtually all of them are college and university educated. Employment opportunities are expected to be good for the next five years. Half the country's engineers earn more than $31,874. The income leaders are in petroleum and mining and average $38,000, followed by chemicals at $35,000, nuclear at $34,200, and aerospace at $33,800.

Ceramicists and Ceramic Engineers: Dishes and teapots may come to mind, but ceramics actually means nonmetal, inorganic substances that have to be processed at high temperatures. While iron ore and french fries are excluded, this category includes practically everything else, from glassware to furnace linings, electronic components, nuclear reactors, and, if it's enamel, the kitchen sink. Ceramic engineers not only design the systems for manufacturing these products but also the factories and equipment in which the work is done.

There are about fourteen thousand ceramic engineers, most of them in the stoneware, clay, and glass industries. This is a profession for the future; it is expected to grow faster than most due to wide use of ceramic materials in nuclear energy production, electronics, defense, and medical science. Another growing area is the development of filters and catalytic surfaces to reduce bacterial contaminants and improve fluid purity.

The average income for a ceramic engineer is about $30,000 per year. The least lucrative jobs are in production, where the average income is $26,100, while the most lucrative is in management, earning an average $38,600 per year.

Chemical Engineers: Chemical engineers may be the alchemists of the New Age. As we deplete our natural reserves of minerals and fossil fuels, we need to develop new processes for retrieving these valuable substances. Already, towns are looking with interest at their garbage, as chemical engineers experiment with processes for separating out the reusable elements of what used to be called waste.

Chemical engineering is a highly specialized field. Most of the fifty thousand chemical engineers work intensively on one kind of process, such as oxidation or polymerization, or on one type of chemical product. They design the equipment and plants in which these products are manufactured and figure out how to mechanize a chemical process on a larger than laboratory scale.

The chemicals industry is expected to continue expanding in coming decades, requiring the services of growing numbers of these highly trained professionals. Necessary background for the field is a thorough grounding not only in chemistry but also in the related disciplines of physics and mechanical and electrical engineering. Chemical engineering is one of the best paid branches of engineering, with engineers earning an average $35,000 per year.

Civil Engineers: The ancient Romans who designed the aqueducts were civil engineers, as were the builders of the pyramids. This is the oldest branch of the engineering profession and the achievement record to date is excellent. The fountains of Rome are still gushing, the pyramids are standing, and London Bridge still hasn't fallen down (although it has been moved to Lake Havasu City, Arizona).

Civil engineers design and supervise construction of roads, harbors, airports, tunnels, bridges, water supply and sewage systems, as well as buildings. Major specialties include structural, hydraulic, environmental, transportation, and geotechnical engineering and soil mechanics. Most civil engineers (there are some 155,000) work for government agencies or private construction companies. Some also work for consulting engineering and architectural firms or as independent consulting engineers. The latter may move from place to place and throughout the world to work on various projects.

This is a growing occupation and future job opportunities are good in housing and industrial building, electric power generating plants, and transportation systems, and in the newer fields of environmental pollution control and alternative energy production. In general, civil engineering pays less than the other branches of engineering. Starting salaries are about $15,500 per year.

FORESTERS

Recent generations knew that trees provided heat in the winter and cool shade in the summer, but they didn't realize that they would ever have to actually take care of one of America's greatest natural resources. Today it is the foresters who are chiefly responsible for the management, development, and protection of United States woodlands. In addition to working with the cutting and planting of trees, foresters may also be responsible for wildlife protection, watershed management, and the supervision of recreational parks and camps. Of the twenty-five thousand foresters in the United States, two out of five work for private industry—paper and lumber companies—while one-fourth work for the federal government's Forest Service. The others work for state and local governments, colleges and universities, or as consultants. Most beginning foresters earn $12,000 a year while experienced foresters average between $18,000 and $21,000.

A bachelor's degree in forestry is the minimum requirement

for both public and private employers, and competition for jobs is increasing. Many employers favor candidates with advanced degrees. Although in recent years there has been an increase in the number of people graduating with forestry degrees, there is still expected to be an increasing demand for foresters in the eighties as the country becomes more keenly aware of the needs both to conserve forests and to develop methods of growing high quality trees in shorter periods of time.

GEOLOGISTS

Geologists study the structure, composition, and history of the earth's crust and specialize in either one or a combination of the three general areas—earth materials, earth processes, and earth history.

Of the thirty-one thousand people working as geologists, more than three-fifths work in private industry, and of that number most of the industrial geologists work for petroleum companies, where most of the action and money are. Almost two-thirds of that number work in five oil- and mineral-bearing states: Texas, California, Louisiana, Colorado, and Oklahoma. However, the geological work world ranges from volcanologists (who study active and inert volcanoes) to astrogeologists (who focus on geological conditions on other planets).

The federal government employs two thousand geologists and colleges and universities employ about ninety-five hundred. A bachelor's degree is adequate for entry into some jobs, but the higher the educational training the greater the likelihood of advancement. In teaching jobs an advanced degree is a must. Employment opportunities, thanks to the increasing concern and need for energy sources, are expected to be very good, especially in the search for fossil fuels and geothermal sources. Graduates in physical and earth sciences are receiving starting salaries of $21,912; a federal geologist earns an average of $26,500.

MATHEMATICIANS

Mathematicians have sought objective truth in an abstract form since the beginning of recorded history. Of course, they have devised systems for visualizing their thoughts—geometric shapes, Phoenician numerals, the abacus, color-coded rods—but the most complex mathematical processes take place unseen inside the human brain and in computers.

Professional mathematicians (thirty-three thousand of them) work either in theoretical (pure) or applied mathematics. Theoretical mathematicians, usually employed by universities, concentrate on research to discover new mathematical principles and formulas. Their findings are often later used in all kinds of scientific endeavors. Applied mathematicians work on solving specific problems in business, economics, computers, engineering, aerospace, natural and social sciences, and linguistics.

Three-quarters of all mathematicians work for colleges and universities teaching the mathematicians and scientists of tomorrow. Most positions in the field require at least a master's degree and preferably a Ph.D. However, jobs are hard to come by even with all that schooling, and competition for openings, particularly in pure math, is expected to increase steadily. Starting salaries range from $14,800 to $25,900, depending on qualifications.

METEOROLOGISTS

The television weatherman is the best-known, but hardly the typical, meteorologist. In fact, synoptic meteorology (weather forecasting) comprises only a third of the field. Physical meteorologists study the atmosphere, its effect on light, sound, and radio waves, and factors affecting the formation of clouds, rain, and snow. Climatologists research the history, trends, and patterns of weather. Still other meteorologists apply weather and climate information to practical problems in fields such as travel, sports, agriculture, industrial operations, and air pollution control.

There are only about seventy-three hundred members of this rarefied profession. Jobs are scattered, but one-fifth exist in just two states: California and Maryland. Almost 10 percent of all meteorologists work in the Washington, D.C., area, the locus of the National Oceanic and Atmospheric Administration (NOAA) and other government departments that use weather and climate information.

Meteorologists earn twice the average for comparable workers. Government salaries average $27,600. Airline meteorologists average between $25,000 and $31,000. Although about a hundred colleges and universities offer programs in meteorology and atmospheric science, it is not essential to specialize in the field so long as one has a science or engineering degree with some credit hours in meteorology. Advanced positions require advanced degrees, but this can often be arranged in conjunction with work. NOAA, which alone employs eighteen hundred meteorologists, has a college study program.

The job outlook, if not absolutely sunny, is nevertheless good for those who are qualified. Jobs in this field are expected to remain relatively static.

OCEANOGRAPHERS

After outer space, the ocean is the world's largest work place—an enormous biological factory covering two-thirds of the earth's surface. Those who work in, on, and under it, studying its denizens and resources, are called oceanographers. Their research extends scientific knowledge of undersea life, chemistry, and geology, and leads to practical innovations like new food sources, mining techniques, improved weather forecasting, and systems of national defense.

Although many of America's thirty-six hundred oceanographers conduct experiments at sea, a great many also work in land-based laboratories, studying and cataloging sea creatures, plotting maps, or using computers to check theories of continental drift.

Some oceanographers are scientists with advanced degrees in marine biology, physics, geology, or chemistry. Others are engineers who supervise underwater construction or electronic experts who design instruments used in oceanographic research. Still others are cartographers who chart the seas, their currents, and the underwater terrain.

Most of these jobs are based in colleges and universities or in the federal government, especially in the navy and in the National Oceanic and Atmospheric Administration (NOAA). Most oceanographers work in states that border the ocean; 40 percent of them are found in California, Maryland, and Virginia.

Although thirty-five colleges and universities offer undergraduate degrees in oceanography or marine science, it is actually preferable to specialize in a more general science and then take graduate training in oceanography at one of the sixty-five universities that offer advanced degrees. It is also a good idea to explore programs at universities that have work/study programs on board ship, and that have major oceanographic research facilities. Job hunting is competitive, and those with a Ph.D. or strong science or engineering background have a better chance of employment.

PETROLEUM AND NATURAL GAS WORKERS

Petroleum and natural gas are formed deep beneath the earth's surface by the decay of organic material (plants and animals) that existed on the earth's surface millions of years ago. Petroleum and natural gas now furnish more than three-quarters of our energy needs.

Exploring for petroleum and natural gas is the first step in the production process. Exploration parties are led by college-educated petroleum geologists, paleontologists, mineralogists, petrologists, and other trained specialists. These people determine where oil or natural gas might be found, but only the digging of a well can prove its existence or nonexistence. Wells are virtually always dug in the same way: rig builders set up a portable drilling rig or tower that supports the machinery and equipment to raise and lower the drilling tools.

Drilling supervisors supervise one or more drilling rigs and supply materials and equipment for the crews. A typical rotary drilling crew has four or five workers: driller, derrick operator, engine operator, and one or two helpers.

Rotary drillers supervise the crew and operate the machinery that controls drilling speed and pressure. They also record operations for the benefit of the geological specialists.

Derrick operators, who are second in command, work on small platforms high on the rig to supervise putting pipe in and out of the well hole. They also operate the pumps that run mud through the pipe.

Roughnecks are rotary drill helpers who guide the pipe into and out of the well hole. Roustabouts are general laborers who do maintenance and construction work. Use of these two terms that have found their way into petroleum industry vernacular would seem to indicate there's little room in the field for ballet students.

Workers in the petroleum and natural gas industry have

been averaging about $8.50 per hour, roughly a dollar more than nonsupervisory workers in private industry. Jobs involve hard work, outdoors, in all kinds of weather, and are concentrated in ten states where drilling is a major industry. For the foreseeable future, workers in this industry will be in great demand as domestic drilling intensifies due to deregulation of oil and gas production. Training periods for the various jobs in the field may vary from two months to two years. The major qualifications are mechanical ability and physical stamina.

PHYSICISTS

Physics addresses the great questions—what it all is, where it all came from, where it's going and how fast. Physicists attempt to discern the structure of the universe and to understand how matter and energy interact. Their natural language is mathematics. In translation their ideas tend toward poetry: the "time warp," the "black hole," the "charmed quark."

Though they seek simplicity, physicists are as caught up in complexity as the rest of us. The volume and intricacy of knowledge dictates the need for specialization. Each of the principal specialties—elementary particle physics; nuclear physics; atomic, electron, and molecular physics; physics of condensed matter; optics, acoustics, and plasma physics; and the physics of fluids—has its own set of subspecialties. To further multiply the possibilities, many aspects of physics closely touch on other sciences, thus giving birth to hybrids such as astrophysics, biophysics, and geophysics.

As in other sciences, pure research often yields practical results, and equipment designed to test arcane hypotheses may end up in the kitchen, as in the case of the microwave oven.

A majority of the forty thousand American physicists work in research, and the rest develop new products for chemical, electrical, aircraft, and missile manufacturers. Frequently, those who teach and do research at universities also do consulting work for industry and government.

A doctoral degree is almost mandatory in this field, and a Ph.D. is worth $23,000 to start in government and industry jobs. A beginning teaching job at a college starts at $13,500. The job outlook is good even though physics is no longer the glamour science it was in the 1950s.

STATISTICIANS

How many people in the United States will have home video systems by 1985? What is the average age at which women marry in the southern states? If a twenty-megaton thermonuclear bomb explodes on a clear day at ground level, how many millions of degrees Fahrenheit would the resulting one-and-a-half-mile-wide fireball be? In a society increasingly organized on mass production, mass trends, and massive events, statisticians are needed to keep track of what's happening and to predict what might happen five years from now.

Using mathematical formulas and computers as their tools, statisticians generally apply their skills in a particular field such as marketing, engineering, science, education, and health. A background in higher mathematics is essential and many professionals have M.A.'s or Ph.D.'s in statistics. Of the twenty-three thousand statisticians currently working, two-thirds are employed by private industry and one-eighth work for the federal government (one of them even figured out these statistics!).

There's an old college saying that if you want to make a point you can always come up with some statistics to prove it. As government and business both continue to rely on measurements for success, the demand for statisticians will steadily increase. Beginners range from $10,500 to $13,014, depending on experience and education, while the overall federal average salary in this field is $26,000.

21

> If you rub elbows with a rich man,
> you'll rub a hole in your sleeve.
> —ANONYMOUS

MECHANICS AND REPAIRERS

FURNITURE UPHOLSTERERS

Did you ever sit down on a nice soft couch and suddenly feel a spring pop up under you? A furniture upholsterer is the person you would call to get that couch back into comfortable shape. Using hand tools in a skilled fashion, upholsterers recondition and recover old furniture. They need an eye for color and detail because part of their job is to make the sofas and chairs look attractive and stylish.

Upholsterers usually learn their trade as apprentices. It takes about three years to learn all of the skills required. More than three-quarters of the twenty-seven thousand working upholsterers own and run or work in small shops of fewer than three people. The starting salary for an apprentice is between $3.25 and $4.50 an hour; skilled workers earn between $6.45 and $10.00. Higher incomes are possible if an upholsterer owns his own shop.

Although more people will be buying upholstered furniture as the population grows, people also tend to buy new furniture rather than repair pieces that break so the demand in this trade is not likely to increase in the coming years.

JEWELERS

If beauty is in the eye of the beholder, then jewelers are lucky indeed. Working with some of the earth's most precious natural materials, jewelers have for thousands of years created refined ornaments that symbolize a man or woman's wealth, marital status, and cultural style. The traditional jeweler not only designed a piece but also made the model, cast it, set the stones, and did the engraving and other detailed handwork. Today these diverse tasks are often divided among specialists.

Many jewelers own or work in jewelry sales and repair shops. Others work in large factories that produce rings, necklaces, and bracelets in quantity. While almost all jewelers learn their skills on the job, it is recommended that beginners work in a factory where they can learn the full range of skills required for an experienced jeweler. The Amalgamated Jewelry, Diamond and Watchcase Workers Union and several manufacturers have set up three- or four-year apprenticeships for various aspects of the craft; these programs usually train people already employed by factories. Several technical schools have both repair and design programs for those who have not already entered the field.

Experienced jewelers—there are about thirty-seven thousand of them—earn from $5 to $7 an hour, but those in business for themselves, and one-third of them are, earn more.

LOCKSMITHS

There is evidence that Egyptian royalty had wooden locks and keys as early as 2000 B.C. More recent advances in the art of safekeeping have been the pin tumbler lock (patented in 1861), the combination lock, the master lock system, and the electronic burglar alarm, an innovation that complicates the lives of not only burglars but also locksmiths, police, and city-dwellers attempting to sleep.

Those wishing to enter this trade should have a high school education and be dexterous, patient, and honest. The best way to learn is to work for a locksmith. But employers will not hire anyone who has a criminal record, and many states require locksmiths to be licensed and fingerprinted. Those entering the trade should also be prepared to spend some sleepless nights running around helping people who have locked themselves out of their cars, homes, and businesses.

Locksmiths earn between $5.00 and $7.50 an hour. Many who are self-employed earn more. Jobs should continue to be plentiful as Americans grow more and more security-conscious.

MECHANICS

What scientists and engineers devise, mechanics are left to maintain and repair. In the opinion of many, a good mechanic is as much an artist as a technician. Scientific theories and engineering blueprints are all well and good, but if the blasted machine doesn't work, one does not go back to the theory or the engineer, one goes to a mechanic: the nuts and bolts man.

A great many mechanics acquire their skills on the job but there is an increasing growth of mechanical trade schools, both within and without the public education system. Wages vary greatly depending upon one's specialty, experience, and job situation (i.e., whether one is an employee or self-employed, and the geographical location of his firm or business).

Appliance Mechanics: Appliance mechanics came into being with the electrification, modernization, and gadgetization of the American home. From toaster to thermostat, from furnace to frying pan, from telephone to television, we depend on mechanics to keep our appliances operating. Most appliance mechanics specialize, of course, because of the nature of the machinery with which they deal. Average hourly wage is $5 to $10 depending on the appliance and its complexity.

Auto Mechanics: More than one-third of the three million mechanics in this country are automotive mechanics. And anyone who owns a car knows a good mechanic is as rare as a Stutz Bearcat and virtually as valuable.

Auto mechanics, good ones, are as much diagnosticians as repairers. Finding the cause of trouble is frequently more important than the remedial actions, which are usually commonly known. Almost anyone can patch a tube; the trick is to find out where the leak is. An auto mechanic's average hourly wage is $9.30.

Business Machine Mechanics: Business machine mechanics help corporations keep up with the paper race. Business machines are now using enough paper yearly to threaten the existence of the Petrified Forest. Almost all business machines use paper: typewriters, adding and calculating machines, cash registers, postage meters, duplicating and copying machines, and even paper shredders (for uncertain or nervous executives). A good percentage of the mechanics in this field are involved in preventive maintenance. They average $200 to $300 a week.

Farm Equipment Mechanics: Farm equipment mechanics is a good business, thanks to the proliferation of suburban and exurban gentlemen farmers who are buying an increasing number of small tractors and lawn mowers that they don't know how to fix. The continual refinement of heavy equipment for serious farming has made combines, harvesters, and tractors too complex for tinkering.

Many mechanics used to enter this field from a related job (farming, auto, or air-conditioning mechanics), but these days technical training in electronics has become more important and many vocational schools and junior and technical colleges offer courses. The armed forces is also a good training ground.

Almost every farm equipment dealership employs some mechanics, and there are many independent repair shops. Manufacturers of heavy farming equipment also employ mechanics, and a few are self-employed. This is a great job for people who want to avoid the urban rat race. On the other hand, there is a kind of rural rat race during planting and harvesting times, when mechanics may work six or seven days a week, ten to twelve hours a day, often driving around to fix machines in the field so that harvesting or threshing can be resumed at once. During winter, mechanics may work less than forty hours a week, and some may be laid off. On the average, farm equipment mechanics are paid $6 per hour.

Vending Machine Mechanics: There are more than five million vending machines in this country and more than twenty-three thousand mechanics servicing them so you won't kick the machines trying to get back your change when they don't drop out your cigarettes or soft drinks.

Vending machine mechanics usually enter the field as shop helpers or route drivers. There are no specific education requirements, and on-the-job training periods vary. Mechanical ability is a requisite. Those who tend vending machines are primarily required to keep the machines in working order, which means they must be capable of taking the machines apart and putting them back together. Because they are sometimes required to restock the vending machines, mechanics may be required to do some clerical work as well. For their efforts, they are paid between $4.25 and $7.25 per hour.

WATCH REPAIRERS

Time may be running out for the classic watch repairman, the bent figure with a loupe in his eye using minuscule tools to loosen and tighten minuscule screws and remove and replace minuscule parts in delicate and expensive watches. The nature of the watch that keeps our time is changing. Mass-produced, electronic watches may well become so inexpensive that it will be cheaper to buy a new one than repair an old one. Solid-state, digital watches have no moving parts and factory technicians can repair them without the expertise of the watch repairman. Nonetheless, a quality watch remains a treasured object and the market for trained watch repairers is expanding, albeit at a slower rate than the average for all occupations.

The nature of the work is intricate and requires patience, manual dexterity, and good eye-hand coordination. Generally, there are no education requirements to enter the watch repair field, and training courses can last from one to three years.

In entry jobs, watch repairmen can earn between $150 and $250 for a forty-hour week. Experienced repairmen can earn up to $350 for the same forty hours: the rate, of course, varies. As long as Tiffany and Cartier sell watches costing $15,000 and much more, the men who repair them will get considerably more than the fellow who works on a Timex.

22

> All progress is based upon a universal innate desire on the part of every organism to live beyond its income.
>
> —SAMUEL BUTLER

HEALTH

CHIROPRACTORS

Chiropractic is a system of medical treatment based on the idea that health is determined by the condition of the nervous system. Parts of the patient's body are manipulated, especially the spine; and water, light, and heat therapy, as well as changes in diet and exercise, are also used. Chiropractors do not prescribe drugs or perform surgery.

Compared with traditional medicine, this is a small field, but it seems to be growing in public acceptance. There are eighteen thousand practicing chiropractors (mostly found in small towns) and fifteen chiropractic colleges, not all of them accredited.

Unlike general medicine, only two years of general college are required before entering chiropractic study. The curriculum is less rigorous than in medical schools, although there is usually some classroom and lab work in anatomy, physiology, and biochemistry, and in physiotherapy and nutrition, in addition to the techniques of manipulation and spinal adjustment. During their last two years of the four-year course, students get practical experience in college clinics. Once they have passed the licensing exam in the state where they plan to practice, they may begin a career by assisting an experienced chiropractor, purchasing an established practice, or simply financing and setting up their own offices.

If present trends continue, enrollment in chiropractic colleges will increase during the 1980s, possibly making it more difficult for new graduates to establish themselves in some areas. Getting good training and finding a receptive community will be important factors in determining individual success. Starting salaries for chiropractors begin at $12,000, but the average salary for the profession is over $25,000.

DENTAL HYGIENISTS AND DENTAL ASSISTANTS

People trained in these two areas of oral health shouldn't have any problem finding work in the eighties; in fact, they'll have their pick of jobs. And they'll be able to choose to work part-time or full-time, in a rural or urban locale.

Dental hygienists must be licensed in order to practice. They may work under the supervision of a dentist or independently. In a dentist's office they clean teeth, apply medicine to prevent tooth decay, take and develop X-rays, record histories, and give instruction on proper dental care. If they work for school systems, hygienists examine and clean children's teeth and educate students on brushing techniques and good eating habits.

Dental assistants work more directly with the dentist as he or she examines the patient's teeth: first they prepare the patient for examination, and then they assist the dentist by placing suction and rubber dams in the patient's mouth. They may also make casts of teeth, process X-ray films, and do secretarial work in the office.

The thirty-five thousand hygienists in the United States are all licensed. In most cases this means that they have graduated from an accredited dental school and passed both a written and a clinical exam. The 182 schools in this field grant degrees ranging from an associate to a master's. They require a high school diploma, and in some instances two years of college, for entry. There are many more dental assistants than hygienists—150,000 in all. Their skills can be learned on the job although there are an increasing number of programs in junior colleges and vocational schools that provide training accredited by the American Dental Association. These programs generally take about a year to complete and may also be pursued through correspondence. Graduates must pass an exam to become certified.

Dental hygienists earn $12,000 to $13,000 a year. Assistants earn an average of between $9,000 and $12,000, depending upon their experience and the locale in which they work.

DENTISTS

Could there possibly be 120,000 people who don't wake up dreading the day they have to go to the dentist's office? There are—all of them dentists—plus another 160,000 who work alongside them, the hygienists and assistants. But constantly improving dental technology is striving to make regular visits more pleasurable for us all. Most dentists have long since given up the "foot on the knee and pliers" technique. Nowadays dental patients can be lulled by the blissful sounds of mellow music in their ears, scenes of a remote beach before their eyes, and the gentle spray of warm water in their open mouths.

Most dentists are in private practice and work as general practitioners. The 10 percent who specialize in orthodontics (straightening teeth), oral surgery (oh, those wisdom teeth!), periodontics (treating inflamed gums), pedodontics (children's dentistry), prosthodontics (making dentures), public health, and oral pathology (diseases of the mouth) receive notably more for their services than a regular dentist.

The regulations governing the practice of dentristry vary from state to state: in all cases dentists need a license to practice. They must graduate from an approved dental school and pass written and clinical examinations. Specialists are required by either the state or the local dental association to have two to three years of graduate education in their chosen areas. New dentists earn an average of $19,300, but the average yearly salary for those in the dental profession is over $50,000.

Entry into dental school is very competitive. Although a bachelor's degree is preferred, it is not required. Dental school takes four academic years, or three full years, to complete with the first two years in the classroom and the last two in clinics. Most schools award the Doctor of Dental Surgery (D.D.S.) but some give the Doctor of Dental Medicine (D.D.M.).

The demand for dentists will increase in the eighties as

public awareness of preventive health care increases. In fact, the number of places in dental schools cannot provide enough dentists for openings, so dentists will be working in a seller's market. Salaries are already high, but there is a wide variation in earnings between those who work in small towns and those in cities.

DIETITIANS

We all know a healthy diet makes us feel better, helps keep our bodies in shape, and helps prevent illness. But what is a healthy diet? Should we take twenty vitamin capsules each morning or be sure to eat spinach three times weekly? Do we all need to eat the same foods? Recently there's been increased public awareness of diet (and diets), but few people know what goes into good nutrition.

Dietitians are the experts in this field. They not only advise the general public on what to eat but also plan meals for large institutions like hospitals, factories, and schools, and they work with individual patients whose physical conditions require very special foods. Dietitians aim to plan a series of meals that are varied, balanced, and appealing to the eater; failing the latter they give the food a glamorous name—"Deep Sea Delight with Milanese Macaroni Supreme."

The thirty-five thousand dietitians in the United States work in administrative, clinical, research, and teaching positions in hospitals, clinics, colleges, schools, large companies, and the armed forces. Most of these food experts hold at least a bachelor's degree and have educational background in nutrition, chemistry, bacteriology, physiology, sociology, and economics. Dietitians accredited by the American Dietetic Association (ADA) receive professional training in an internship program of approximately one year either after graduation or as part of their four years in college. While a public health nutritionist needs a graduate degree, students who have associate degrees from vocational schools and junior colleges are also finding positions as dietitians.

Hospital dietitians receive a starting salary of $12,600 a year, but experienced dietitians range between $15,000 and $30,000 annually. Self-employed dietitians with bachelor's degrees who work as consultants have a median salary of $20,000.

EKG TECHNICIANS

Most of the nation's twenty thousand medical technicians overseeing electrocardiograph machines are employed in hospital centers. While some vocational schools and junior colleges give courses in this medical specialty, many technicians receive on-the-job training. A mastery of the basic EKG tests can be obtained within six months or a year. The starting salary is not exceptional, approximately $7,800 per year according to one survey; but experienced technicians can earn $15,100. They receive the same benefits as all hospital personnel. With the continuing demand for medical services and an increasing number of older citizens, demand for electrocardiographic examinations will outpace normal employment growth. EKG technicians can advance within the hospital structure to become cardiology technologists and departmental supervisors.

EMERGENCY MEDICAL TECHNICIANS

The life of the emergency medical technician is a real adventure saga that rivals the television versions. Working in teams of two, these ambulance attendants zoom to the scene of a medical emergency and immediately administer lifesaving medical aid—making sure the patient can breathe, controlling bleeding, treating shock, burns, and fractures, and managing mentally disturbed patients. Nonmedical skills are also required on some occasions in extricating victims of traffic accidents from their vehicles or controlling a crowd.

Some emergency medical technicians are paramedics, who can administer drugs and operate equipment like a cardiac defibrillator that the average ambulance attendant is not trained to use. Still others are ambulance dispatchers, stationed within a hospital, police, or fire department, where they coordinate emergency services by radio.

Half the nation's EMTs were volunteer members of community rescue squads. The trend is toward replacement of these volunteer squads with paid ambulance services. This tendency, the public demand for quality emergency medical services, and government encouragement for EMT training and certification in community colleges make this one of the fastest growing jobs for the future.

Graduates of approved eighty-one-hour training programs

merit starting salaries between $7,500 and $12,000 a year. Differences in salary scale depend on community size and region, and on the employer. Generally, EMTs working out of fire departments are paid on a scale with fire fighters. They also work longer hours than those who work for police departments, hospitals, or private ambulance companies.

Although it is not necessary for employment, many of the nation's 287,000 EMTs are registered with the National Registry of Emergency Medical Technicians.

LICENSED PRACTICAL NURSES

Licensed practical nurses are responsible for much of the bedside care that patients receive in a hospital, long-term health care facility, or private home. They take temperatures and blood pressures, bathe and feed patients, and assist physicians and R.N.'s in examinations. L.P.N.'s who work in obstetrics may assist with delivery of babies, while those in intensive care units may operate highly sophisticated equipment in treating the seriously ill. L.P.N.'s who work for private patients may prepare meals and teach members of the family how to perform basic nursing tasks.

Of the 518,000 L.P.N.'s, three-fifths work in hospitals. Many others are employed by public health agencies and welfare organizations as well as nursing homes, clinics, and private doctors.

An L.P.N. must complete a year of training and pass a state examination. Training is offered in trade, technical, and vocational schools, junior colleges, local hospitals, and health agencies. Although most schools prefer candidates who have completed high school, they also accept those without a diploma. Required courses for an L.P.N. include anatomy, pediatrics, obstetrics, first aid, nutrition, and psychiatric nursing. The accompanying clinical experience is most often in a hospital.

L.P.N.'s can work part-time and continue to study in R.N. programs if they wish. They earn an average beginning salary of $9,100, and although they usually work forty hours a week, these hours include night, weekend, and holiday shifts.

MEDICAL LABORATORY WORKERS

All medical occupations are expected to grow in the coming decades, but medical laboratory workers will be in the greatest demand, with an estimated twenty thousand jobs opening up each year, more than half of them new positions.

Doctors are making ever greater use of tests and laboratory analysis in making diagnoses and determining treatment. The lab staff, working under the supervision of a pathologist or physician, consists of three levels of workers: medical technologists, technicians, and assistants.

An assistant's job requires only one year of formal training, and the work is fairly routine—storing, labeling, cleaning, sterilizing, record keeping. Technicians must have two years of post-secondary training, since their jobs involve more complicated lab procedures. The medical technologist has four years of training and performs complex chemical, microscopic, and bacteriological tests. In large laboratories, technologists often specialize in microbiology, parasitology, biochemistry, blood banking, hematology, and nuclear medical technology. In a small lab, the technologist may be expected to know something of all these areas.

There are about 210,000 medical laboratory workers. Most of them work in hospital labs, but others work in independent laboratories, physicians' offices, clinics, public health agencies, pharmaceutical firms, and research institutions. The highest paying jobs are on the West Coast and in large cities.

Although the work does involve contact with germs and diseased tissue, which has some unpleasant aspects, medical laboratories are clean, and special handling methods virtually eliminate health hazards.

The average salary for laboratory assistants is $11,400; for medical technicians it is $13,500; for medical technologists the annual average is $15,700.

MEDICAL RECORD TECHNICIANS

It seems bad enough to get sick without having to keep a record of it, but the fact is there is as much paper as medicine moving around the average hospital these days. All medical records are permanent—at least for the patient's lifetime—and the task of transcribing appropriate data, coding the information, filing and maintaining registries, and then making use of the aggregate information as medical statistics requires special training.

There are sixty-six two-year college programs that culminate in an associate degree of medical record science and qualify their graduates for certification by the American Medical Record Association as accredited record technicians (ARTs). The association also offers a correspondence course in medical transcription that prepares those who complete it for entry-level jobs as medical record clerks.

Advancement possibilities in this highly specialized and growing field are good. Clerks can advance to the technical level through various education programs and those who train as technicians can expect promotion to supervisory positions as their expertise increases. Earnings for both clerks and technicians vary according to locality. The average pay for beginning clerks in private hospitals is $8,400, but the range is from $6,600 in small southern hospitals to $13,200 in New York City. Technicians' salaries follow the same regional patterns. The beginning salaries in federal hospitals start at $8,400 and average about $11,200.

NURSING AIDES, ORDERLIES, AND ATTENDANTS

Male and female nursing aides, orderlies, and attendants are responsible for most of the nonmedical care patients receive in hospitals and nursing homes, including serving meals, feeding, dressing, and bathing patients, taking temperatures, and assisting patients to walk. Aides are trained on the job under the supervision of registered and licensed practical nurses. While a high school diploma may be required, many institutions simply seek people who are sympathetic and dependable.

Nursing aides' wages vary a great deal, with hospitals usually paying higher salaries than nursing homes. The average salary paid by the federal government to aides is $205 a week, and it is about the same in private hospitals and homes.

Since patients require twenty-four-hour care, aides may work afternoon or evening shifts as well as some weekends and holidays. This is a growing field, particularly in the area of convalescent homes and long-term care facilities. There are already one million people working in these positions today.

OCCUPATIONAL THERAPISTS

As both the public and the health professionals become increasingly aware that pills and potions will not cure all of our health problems, there is greater demand for both preventive and therapy techniques in medicine. Occupational therapists are part of this movement and their work with the ill and the disabled is aimed at strengthening old skills and developing new ones. Devising games for handicapped children or those with learning disabilities, using theater improvisation with elderly residents of a nursing home, or teaching the blind to type are a few examples of the educational, vocational, and recreational activities that their work involves. Therapists need to be creative, flexible, and patient so that they are able to adapt to each patient's physical and emotional capacity.

The fifteen thousand occupational therapists in the United States are assisted by almost as many occupational therapy assistants and aides. A registered occupational therapist (OTR) must complete a degree program to be certified by both the American Medical Association and the American Occupational Therapy Association. The degree can be obtained through a four-year course that includes a bachelor's degree or in a shorter certificate course for students who already have a bachelor's in another field. A master's in occupational therapy is necessary for teaching, research, and administrative positions. All of the occupational therapy programs include course work in the sciences as well as six to nine months of clinical work in hospitals or health agencies.

Therapy assistants may attend a two-year college program that culminates in an associate degree. If they pass a proficiency exam they become certified occupational therapy assistants (COTA), and this designation, along with four years of work experience, entitles them to take the OTR exam. Occupational therapy aides learn on the job. They perform a broad range of tasks from teaching crafts to teaching the use of power tools that develop skills and stimulate patients on their road back to a healthy life.

While this field is growing, the increasing number of graduates who choose this specialty may make competition in the next few years fairly stiff. Many occupational therapy positions are part-time. Salaries for a registered occupational therapist range from $13,000 for a beginner to $22,000 for an experienced OTR. Salaries for administrative positions range from $25,000 to $30,000. Occupational therapy assistants earn from

$9,000 to $11,000 before they have experience, but then move up to $12,500. Aides earn an average of $7,500 a year.

OPTOMETRISTS

The twenty-one thousand practicing optometrists are responsible for examining, evaluating, and prescribing eyeglasses and contact lenses to persons in need of vision correction. Since so many people require glasses, and fashion has made an impact on this field, optometrists are doing a land-office business.

To practice optometry all states require a formal educational program, usually resulting in a Doctor of Optometry, before issuing a license. Optometrists, in a sense, bridge the eye field since their work overlaps with the ophthalmologist, the physician of eye diseases, and the optician, the dispenser of glasses. Most optometrists are self-employed, operating retail shops or optical departments in large stores. For new optometrists, average earnings are likely to be in the neighborhood of $16,200; however, experienced optometrists earn an average of $40,000. Federal government optometrists earn an average of $22,700.

PHARMACISTS

The profession of druggist has come a long way from dispensing garlic and wine to be rubbed on the skull in case of headache—a biblical remedy. Today there are over 135,000 licensed pharmacists; about half own their own drugstores, and the most common thing they dispense in those stores is film rather than drugs. Nevertheless, pharmacies are the major source of medicine and makeup, perfume and shaving cream, powders and prophylactics.

To become a licensed druggist one must take a five-year course in one of the seventy-three accredited colleges and pass a state board examination. In general, states tend to recognize other states' licenses. While many pharmacists work in hospitals, earning an average $17,500, most work in drugstores where they usually earn over $21,000. Druggists owning their own shops are better paid, but then that is due to profits as well as prescriptions. Given the passion with which Americans take medicine (about $68 worth of pills per year per person) and welcome new drugs, it appears to be a continuing growth area.

PHYSICIANS

The necessity of going through ten years of schooling and clinical work, often in intellectually competitive and physically grueling situations, calls for individuals who are determined, dedicated, and diligent. But they probably wouldn't even have made it into medical school if they weren't. And they probably wouldn't have chosen this career if they hadn't been well aware of the glorification that our culture bestows on them in the long run.

Averaging over $60,000 a year for unincorporated physicians and over $80,000 for incorporated ones, physicians have the highest annual incomes in the country. They not only command high fees, but they also have very good job security. Of the 450,000 practicing doctors, 90 percent work in patient care including offices and hospitals, while 28,000 work in administration and research. These days most practitioners specialize in the following seven areas: general practice, internal medicine, general surgery, psychiatry, obstetrics and gynecology, pediatrics, and anesthesiology (in descending order of popularity). But there are three dozen fields of specialization.

Initiation into the medical profession involves a long series of difficult courses, examinations, and work in labs and hospitals. First, in order to get into one of the 116 accredited medical schools in the United States, you need a strong academic background, particularly in the sciences, superior letters of recommendation, and extracurricular experiences, such as volunteer work in an emergency room or assistance in a cancer research lab, that indicate a real interest in this field. In addition, high scores on the Medical College Admission Test are a prerequisite. Even with all of these qualifications, only one-third of all applicants find places in U.S. medical schools.

Once admitted, however, medical students are given tremendous support (financial and academic) as they work through four years of a rigorous curriculum. Schools vary in that some include work with patients in the first years while others wait until course work is nearly completed. In all cases, after finishing the classroom material, students serve a one- or two-year residency in a hospital where they are exposed to all aspects of medicine. Then, if they choose to become certified in a specialty, they go on for two to four years in a residency in that field. After completing residency, prospective M.D.'s must pass a national test to obtain a license allowing them to practice. On the average, doctors work a sixty-two-hour week, and contrary to popular belief only 11 percent play golf. The job outlook is cloudy since the country is heading for an oversupply—perhaps a surplus of thirty-five thousand physicians by 1990. In addition, the health care delivery system may change in coming years. The saturation of urban areas with M.D.'s may force some new doctors to move to rural communities, and the high cost of medical care may eventually force the nation into some kind of public health system.

PODIATRISTS

The word *psyche* is derived from the Greek word for "mind." So a psychiatrist is someone who specializes in problems of the mind. The word *pod* is derived from the Greek meaning "foot," so a podiatrist is someone who specializes in problems of the foot. In between there are other specialists, because modern medicine would have us protected head to foot.

A podiatrist diagnoses and treats foot diseases and deformities. He takes X-rays, performs surgery, prescribes drugs, fits corrective devices, and supervises physical therapy.

There are more than eighty-one hundred people practicing podiatry in this country, most of them self-employed, and their average yearly income is over $40,000, with starting salaries averaging $19,260.

To get into a school of podiatric medicine requires three years of college, and the course takes four years, two of them in classroom instruction and two more involving practical clinical experience and continued academic study.

Experts in the field recommend that aspirants have both scientific aptitude and manual dexterity. Congeniality, they say, is also an asset. So put your best foot forward.

PSYCHOLOGISTS

This large and ever-expanding profession (ninety thousand at last count) is bent on understanding and explaining human behavior, with a view to straightening some of it out.

There are at least fifteen different kinds of psychologists. Clinical psychologists are the largest group (40 percent of the total). Working in mental hospitals or clinics, they counsel the mentally disturbed and their families. Although some of the techniques of psychotherapy may be used, psychologists also rely on direct methods like behavior modification. They generally try to improve the patient's adjustment to everyday life rather than delving into his inner world.

A great many psychologists work in the laboratory—often within the university—conducting experiments with rats, cats, primates, and humans, in order to better understand neurological processes such as motivation, learning, and sensory perception. A great many psychologists are being employed these days by business and industry to improve on-the-job performance and interaction among employees. Still others work exclusively with children or with senior citizens.

This is a fast-growing field, but there will be keen competition for the top jobs, which require a doctorate in psychology. The most promising opportunities will be in the applied areas of clinical, counseling, industrial, or organizational psychology rather than in the more traditional fields of experimental, physiological, and comparative psychology. The applied specialties also bring the highest salaries. There are good jobs for psychologists with the federal government in the areas of education and human resources. For psychology students, some financial help in the form of fellowships and low-interest loans is available through the Veterans Administration intern program, the National Science Foundation, the Department of Education, and the armed forces. The starting salary for psychologists is between $10,700 and $13,200, while the average salary is $24,000 for those with a Ph.D.

REGISTERED NURSES

Nurses are the healers who provide the steady care and attention that help patients to recover from illness. Ministering to the sick person's daily needs, monitoring his/her daily progress and change, dispensing medications, arranging flowers, talking with the family, and making a fuss over new babies, nurses nourish their patients with an environment of real human strength and support. While three-quarters of the total one million nurses work in hospitals, where they specialize in a particular area such as surgery or pediatrics, others work in offices assisting physicians. Community health programs and large industries also need nurses to serve as occupational health workers. Still others are employed as private duty nurses who care for a single patient. A significant number also teach in nursing schools.

Registered nurses are distinguished from other kinds of nurses in that they have more medical education and a professional license that permits them to dispense medications, change dressings and I.V.'s, and make some kinds of medical decisions in emergencies. There are three types of basic nursing school programs, all of which require a high school degree for entry. Diploma programs set up by hospitals and independent nursing schools usually last three years and simply provide the graduate with a nursing school certificate. Bachelor's degree programs in colleges and universities take four to five years to complete but the student finishes with both a B.S. and a nursing diploma. Associate degree programs in junior colleges provide two years of nursing education. After going through any of these schooling programs a nurse must pass a state test in order to practice.

Beyond this initial training there are now many master's and doctoral programs that enable a nurse to work in research, teaching, clinical specializations, and supervisory positions in hospitals.

Nursing is a growing field, both in numbers and in responsibility. The "nurse-practitioner" program offered in many states enables a nurse to do routine medical examinations and to have a more independent role in administering primary care.

Nurses working in hospitals average $13,700 a year while those employed by the federal government earn an average of $16,800. Self-employed nurses can work by the day or on a part-time basis on one of the three eight-hour shifts.

SPEECH PATHOLOGISTS

Speech therapists are now generally required to have advanced training, usually a master's degree, in order to be licensed by some states or if they fall within the jurisdiction of a Medicaid or Medicare program. These federal programs have created a substantial number of job opportunities in recent years. Consequently, there are thirty-eight thousand speech pathologists and audiologists (specialists in hearing disorders), and the number promises to grow.

Salaries of speech therapists vary, depending on whether they are attached to a hospital, clinic, school, or are in private practice. The starting salary in federal jobs is $14,300 for therapists with master's degrees and $19,300 for those with doctorates. For all speech and audio therapists, salaries paid by federal agencies average $24,300. In private practice speech pathologists charge between $15 and $20 per session. There is a large audience for these services, for it is estimated that one out of ten Americans cannot speak or hear clearly.

VETERINARIANS

A man's best friend is said to be his dog. But a dog's best friend could well be his veterinarian. Unless one lives in a rural area, one's concept of a doctor of veterinary medicine is a "pet" doctor; indeed, more than 30 percent of the 33,500 vets in this country do focus their practice on pets.

Actually, veterinarians diagnose, treat, and control diseases and attend to injuries of animals both large and small, from the hippopotamus to the hamster, from the mouse to the moose. One important function of the veterinarian is to prevent the spread of animal diseases among a herd of cattle, for instance, or a flock of chickens. Some animal diseases are also serious threats to the health of human beings, and arresting them is the veterinarian's responsibility.

A Doctor of Veterinary Medicine degree requires six years of college, two years of preveterinarian study, and four years of professional work. New graduates have been employed by the federal government at $18,000 per year. The average annual salary of federally employed vets is about $27,300. A high percentage of veterinarians are self-employed and they, of course, earn whatever their patient's owners can afford to pay.

X-RAY TECHNOLOGISTS

X-ray technologists are being thrown more than a bone these days. Technologists operate X-ray equipment and take X-ray pictures, but no longer merely of bone fractures. The X-ray is now used to diagnose lung diseases, stomach ulcers, brain tumors, and other organic ailments. It is also used as therapy, primarily to arrest malignant growths within the body. And in nuclear medicine, X-rays trace the course of radioactive liquids through the body to locate the centers of diseased tissue.

To enter the field, one must be a high school graduate and complete a formal education program in X-ray technology. Starting salaries are about $10,700 a year, and experienced technologists can earn $13,500 or more.

The field for technologists is expanding more rapidly than the average; however, the number of people going into the field is multiplying. Job prospects are good, but aspirants may face increasing competition for choice appointments during the next five years.

23

> The universal regard for money is the
> one hopeful fact in our civilization.
> —GEORGE BERNARD SHAW

SOCIAL SCIENCE

ANTHROPOLOGISTS

Most of the nation's seven thousand anthropologists work for colleges and universities. The rest, about a fifth of the total, work for the federal government. Virtually all contemporary anthropologists, whether they be archaeologists, ethnologists, or linguistic or medical anthropologists, are university-trained, with M.A. or Ph.D. degrees. Since anthropology is the study of people, there is no end of specialized subfields. Outside of teaching, the work can be difficult: living in the field among primitive peoples in adverse circumstances over long periods of time is trying. Anthropologists suffer from cultural shock as much as from isolation. It is a job for very dedicated people.

An anthropologist with a doctorate can expect to begin a professional teaching career earning $16,000 a year. Experienced professionals earn between $18,000 and $30,000 a year. The government pays anthropologists an average of $31,200 a year.

While new applications are developing for anthropological training, employment prospects are not bright as long as college enrollment is static.

ECONOMISTS

"Economics is extremely useful as a form of employment for economists," said noted practitioner John Kenneth Galbraith. Economists are concerned with how society uses its resources. They analyze the relationship between the supply and demand of goods and services. Money, how it moves and how it is valued, is only part of the equation. Economists are just as likely to be thinking about oil or peanuts, the price of wheat, mortgage rates, credit, or the stock market. Some spend all their time just thinking about employment and unemployment, or tariffs and international trade policy. Some think big and worry about the whole picture: macroeconomists. Others think small and examine the parts: microeconomists.

Economists work in colleges and universities (teaching theory, writing research papers, and consulting with government and private corporations); in government (designing tax, trade, and other economic policies); and for business firms (advising management on how to market and price its product). Of 130,000 jobs, three out of four are in the private realms. Academia and government each account for 10 percent, and a few economists are private consultants.

Students looking ahead to careers as economists should be aware that a bachelor's degree will rarely suffice to begin a serious career. They must decide on a specialty before entering graduate school and then select a university that is strong in that area.

Big specialties for the eighties are sure to include quantitative analysis of business trends, the complexities of international commerce, sales forecasting, and planning. Those well trained in econometrics and statistics should be a few points up to start. So should those who specialize in the environment, energy and natural resources, health, and transportation. Teaching positions in colleges and universities are not expected to increase. The average graduate will find happier hunting in business and government.

This is a well-paid profession. Bachelor's degrees in finance and economics entitle recent graduates to somewhat higher starting salaries than the average for other social sciences ($10,600 compared to $10,000). Average salaries of economists in colleges and universities range between $12,100 for instructors and $25,400 for a full professor.

POLITICAL SCIENTISTS

In addition to advising presidents on foreign policy, political scientists have been known to survey public opinion and publish the results, write books, and teach undergraduates about the history of diplomacy and the intricacies of domestic politics. A few of them consult with business firms or study legislation for private groups and public agencies. Every congressman has several on his staff. The U.S. Department of State is a major employer of political scientists, as is the Energy Research and Development Agency, the CIA, A.I.D., the departments of Defense, Treasury, Justice, and Commerce.

Political science has one of the least halcyon employment outlooks for the 1980s except for those who specialize in areas like economics, transportation, health care delivery, and environmental concerns. But even here, competition is expected to be stiff, and many Ph.D.'s may be forced to accept part-time, temporary assignments in lieu of university appointments with tenure. Training in policy making, public administration, and quantitative research methods will also help give some candidates an edge.

There are about fourteen thousand political scientists, 80 percent of them based in colleges and universities. Government employees work in and around Washington, D.C., and abroad. Full professors can expect to make a median salary of $22,000. Political scientists working for the government average about $25,800 to $32,900 a year.

SOCIOLOGISTS

The first law of sociology is: Some do, some don't. Sociology is remarkable not only for the terminology it has invented (two is not a crowd, it's a dyad) but also for the number of bad jokes it inspires, most of them told by sociologists.

In addition to a sense of humor and a flair for professional jargon, the successful sociologist must have a high tolerance for study and research, statistics and computers, and a genuine interest in groups (a group being anything from a married couple to a baseball team, remote tribe, the residents of a housing project, or the gang at the office).

Sociologists specialize in such areas as social organization, social pathology and psychology, rural or urban sociology, criminology and penology, demography, industrial sociology, and medical sociology. Although four-fifths of the nineteen thousand sociologists work in academia, there are increasing numbers employed in private industry and government, advising lawmakers on social problems, working in hospitals and in advertising and marketing. These practical applications of sociological information promise the greatest career opportunities for the future. This is a field that is growing more slowly than most. Those holding a Ph.D. may find it difficult to gain academic positions, although opportunities do exist in business administration and government research, especially in urban studies, ethnic studies and race relations, deviant behavior, community development, population analysis, medical sociology, and the sociology of law, work, and education. Academic sociologists start work earning between $10,500 and $13,000 if they possess B.A.'s, but as much as $19,200 if they hold doctoral degrees. The average faculty sociologist earns $23,000, while the federal government's average is $25,000. Ph.D. sociologists in the federal bureaucracy earn $33,000.

URBAN PLANNERS

Urban planners are paid to advise community officials about how to adjust to growth or decay trends in their areas. With their expertise, they attempt to anticipate future patterns of development in a given community. For instance, they will recommend the expansion or reduction of health facilities, schools, road construction, and so on, based on projected growth patterns. They will also be involved in suggesting resolutions to foreseeable problems, whether social, economic, or environmental. The future is their present and the computer is their crystal ball.

A master's degree in urban planning is the usual requirement for entry into the field, although there are exceptions. Candidates for government jobs must pass civil service tests. Most of the seventeen thousand urban and regional planners work for local or regional agencies, but state and federal agencies appear to be the growing area. Starting salaries range from $13,500 to $15,920. Planning directors at the state level get anywhere from $25,000 to $30,000 a year, but the average salary for a planner is $20,500. The federal government pays an average of $27,450.

24

> The moral flabbiness born of the exclusive worship of the bitch-goddess SUCCESS. That—with the squalid cash interpretation put on the word success—is our national disease.
>
> —WILLIAM JAMES

SOCIAL SERVICE

CAREER PLACEMENT COUNSELORS

Some people make a career out of helping other people make career decisions. Career planning and placement counselors work with students, finding occupations that suit their talents and preferences and then taking some of the anxiety out of the actual job-hunting experience. They aid in writing résumés, arranging job recruitment on campus, communicating with potential employers, and counseling the student on a positive personal presentation in the job interview. Increasingly, placement counselors are being hired in private industry to smooth job changes and assist in the hiring and firing process.

There are about four thousand placement counselors, most of them working in four-year colleges and universities. Training in the behavioral sciences of psychology or sociology is the usual route to career counseling. Although a bachelor's degree is generally acceptable for entry-level jobs, a master's degree may become de rigueur in the future, since candidates for these positions are expected to increase at the same rate as job opportunities. A specialty, such as counseling middle-aged students planning career changes or helping to place handicapped people, may also distinguish an aspiring candidate.

Salaries vary, depending on the size and nature of the institution—factors that also greatly affect possibilities for promotion into higher level administrative positions. The average salary for all career placement jobs is $18,100 per year.

CLERGY

Periods of uncertainty, tension, and anxiety are often periods of religious revivals. This seems to be the case today with a resurgence in attendance and intensity of belief in all three major faiths. Consequently, careers in the clergy are both available and in demand compared to a decade ago when anticlericalism and religious alienation were more common.

Though spiritual and moral guidance is the principal role of a cleric, each faith has its own special theology and biblical interpretation, and naturally its own theological schools. All but the most fundamentalist fringe churches require lengthy training at an accredited institute.

Protestantism has the most followers of the three major faiths, though it is made up of several denominations such as Baptists, Episcopalians, Lutherans, Methodists, and Presbyterians. Nearly 200,000 ministers are employed to tend the needs of 300,000 churches and 72 million worshipers. Ministers in the above denominations have an average salary of $15,500, somewhat higher than the salaries of the ministers of the fundamentalist churches. However, the born-again Christian movement has brought an influx of members and a great deal of money to the churches that are identified with this revivalism. Consequently, the employment outlook for the evangelical denominations is quite formidable.

Roman Catholic priests receive similar training but have different duties. Some are assigned parishes by their bishops to carry out the sacramental duties in their churches, while others belong to religious orders, such as the Jesuits, to fulfill special missions such as teaching or missionary work. Diocesan priests receive minimal salaries, ranging from $2,500 to $7,000 a year plus a rectory room and free board. Members of the religious orders are frequently sworn to poverty and live in communal circumstances. (Nevertheless, Bishop Fulton J. Sheen, a Jesuit, left an estate worth $50,000.)

Catholic clergy are in short supply to attend to the religious needs of the nation's fifty million Catholics. Since seminary training takes eight years, providing for the growing needs of Roman Catholics means that for the foreseeable future there will be a strong demand for men of the cloth.

The smallest of the major religions is Judaism, with approximately 5.7 million Jews, something less than 3 percent of the population. Judaism is divided into three sects of roughly equal size—Orthodox, Conservative, and Reform—with about four thousand ordained rabbis overall. The course of study for rabbinical ordination takes between three and five years. There is a direct correlation between the size and location of the synagogue congregation and the salary it pays its rabbi. While Orthodox rabbis receive the lowest salaries, rabbis generally average between $15,000 and $20,000 a year, often including housing and other benefits. Older and experienced rabbis are paid between $35,000 and $60,000 a year, plus honorariums and fees from officiating at private ceremonies.

GUIDANCE COUNSELORS

In their work with high school students, guidance counselors not only help with career and educational choices but also assist with family and community problems, which seem to be a central part of life during high school years. Counselors are charged with a great responsibility, and they're generally paid more for it than are teachers. The salary of a school counselor ranges from $9,200 to $30,500, but the average salary is close to $18,000.

There are forty-five thousand guidance counselors in the high schools of America. They all have had to meet state regulations that require either a teaching and counseling certificate or just a counseling certificate. A counseling certificate itself may require an M.A. in counseling plus teaching experience, depending on the state. The two things that do not vary are the need for a bedside manner and an insight into people's motivation.

JOB ANALYSTS

Getting the best possible employees available has become an increasingly important job for both industry and government. Analyzing and defining the job requirements and worker characteristics has become very exacting. These analysts prepare descriptions that tell you about the duties of the job and what training and skills it requires.

Of the 405,000 people working in personnel and labor relations nearly three out of four work in private industry. The proportion of job analysts is the same. Some employers look for graduates who have majored in personnel administration or industrial and labor relations. Others prefer college graduates with a general business background and still others, a liberal arts grounding. For government service a major in personnel administration, political science, or public administration might be "one leg up." At least two hundred colleges and universities have programs leading to a labor relations degree.

The need for personnel workers is expected to grow through the mid-eighties. In private industry job analysts begin at $12,000, while the average analyst makes $22,600. In the federal government the starting salary is $10,000, but an analyst with a master's degree can start at $15,300. The average salary in federal work ranges between $21,400 and $33,800.

LABOR RELATIONS

In a small business, you can still ask the boss for a raise and probably get it. But a big corporation is another matter. All employ teams of professionals to negotiate with unions who are themselves often represented by labor relations experts. If everybody disagrees, there is nothing to do but call in an independent arbitrator.

As this increasingly familiar scenario would indicate, the largest employers of trained labor relations personnel are private industry and the federal government. Unions offer some jobs, mainly on the education staffs of their national headquarters. And a few labor relations experts are in business for themselves.

In addition to wage negotiations, labor relations workers deal with the day-to-day enforcement of contracts, employee grievances, and retirement plans. They must keep up with trends in economics, labor law, and wage settlements in related fields. Government labor relations jobs are more likely to involve job analysis and wage classification, setting up and scoring civil service examinations, and enforcing equal opportunity hiring practices.

More than two hundred colleges have programs leading to a

degree in personnel administration, but the number specializing in labor relations is quite small. In general, a B.A. in business administration, political science, or industrial psychology followed by a master's in industrial relations or a law degree is excellent training.

This is a fast-growing field and jobs pay well, so competition will be keen. Salaries for middle level administrators are more than $20,000 a year, with executives earning considerably more.

SOCIAL WORKERS/CASEWORKERS

As the streets of any big city readily show, the wonders of modern civilization have not eliminated the most common and pressing social problems. Although these problems affect individuals, they are generally accepted as a public concern. Social workers are the people who are paid to help solve them. Some deal on a one-to-one basis with other people's troubles (caseworkers); others deal with groups like teenagers or poor people (group workers); still others (community organizers) try to fight social problems at the community or national level by coordinating the activities of large groups or designing policy.

Of the 385,000 social workers employed, most work for government agencies and private institutions. But a growing number are in private practice, offering their counseling services direct to the public for a fee. Because of the complexity and specialized information needed to bring about action, both in individual lives and in the bureaucracies through which help is provided, careers in social work tend to be highly specialized.

A caseworker may concentrate on family and child service or on work with the aged, both fast-growing fields. The specialty in turn affects the place of employment. Although many caseworkers report daily to government offices or charitable organizations, many also work within schools, hospitals, prisons, or mental institutions, or from storefront offices in neighborhoods with special problems.

Whatever the setting or specialty, there are human lives at stake. It is important for social workers not only to be thoroughly trained, with college as a clear necessity, but also to be emotionally mature themselves, and to have a genuine concern for people and their problems.

Nearly half the states have licensing laws. The title A.C.S.W.

(Academy of Certified Social Workers) can be used only by those with two years of job experience who have passed a special examination given by the National Association of Social Workers.

Perhaps unfortunately, this is a burgeoning field. The potential development of national health insurance, expanded educational services, growing numbers of aged, and the need for counseling on everything from consumerism to rape all promise to sustain this growth through the 1980s. Ironically, high unemployment rates in other fields serve to buoy this profession.

This positive outlook for social work employment has increased enrollment in the more than 170 college undergraduate programs and 80 graduate schools of social work. This may mean stiff competition for entry-level jobs in the 1980s, particularly in big cities with fiscal problems. Small towns and rural areas offer less money to start (and fewer colleagues with whom to talk shop) but these may be the most promising places for the beginning social worker to look.

Earnings vary: a social worker with a graduate degree (such as a Master of Social Work) commands up to $16,000 to start, and one with a B.S.W., about $10,300. Top salaries for experienced workers and supervisors are in the $25,000 range.

25

The rich will do everything for the poor
but get off their backs.
—KARL MARX

PERFORMING ARTS, DESIGN, COMMUNICATIONS

ACTORS AND ACTRESSES

The place for studying and working in the acting profession is New York City, home of most acting schools, Broadway, off-Broadway, TV networks, and casting for road productions. The hard fact of how few actors actually manage to support themselves contrasts with the ease and glory associated with big stars.

Many are called but few are chosen. An independent source of income from a free-lance job with flexible hours feeds the body while the soul is auditioning. Trade papers announce "open calls," summer stock theaters, supper clubs, and other opportunities.

Advertising agencies often have open days for casting commercials. An actor or actress can leave a picture and résumé and hope for the best. Because a play is a joint effort of many creative people, it's necessary to have an even disposition and an ability to take direction. A scornful attitude assures a short career.

A painter or writer can work alone, but an actor cannot, so it is important to stay in practice through acting classes or showcases and benefits, that is, unpaid work. There is great camaraderie among those who manage to stick with it, and old acquaintances from acting groups, road shows, school, and so on are remembered and greeted warmly. No work is looked down upon by professionals, and sometimes the very hardships of an early job are the basis for an entertaining evening of storytelling at an actor's bar or party.

The unions—Actors' Equity Association, Screen Actors Guild, Screen Extras Guild, and American Federation of Television and Radio Artists (AFTRA)—assure their members of fair wages when there is work. Unfortunately, the union dues continue regardless of employment status. Three-quarters of the members of Equity and SAG earned less than $2,500 last year. The members are covered by hospitalization and get paid vacations and sick leave.

ADVERTISING/MEDIA SPECIALISTS

As the adman said, "Don't sell the steak, sell the sizzle." Indeed, the first advertisement may well have been the smell of meat cooking over a Paleolithic fire. Today, the hard sell and the soft sell surround us in many media: words, pictures, and commercials, store-window displays, posters in subway stations, point-of-purchase gimmicks, leaflets handed out by pretty women, and pitches disguised as personal mail.

If anything, the art of advertising has become more of a science in recent years. Media specialists who are paid to reach a particular clientele with a product or service have a great deal of information about how to do it efficiently. Market research determines who is most likely to use a product and what these people's habits, preferences, and opinions are. Given this information, the creative team—usually a copywriter, an art director, and various assistants, all under the direction of an account executive—pulls together an advertising campaign designed to sell the product to the right people. Time and space buyers know precisely which media, at which times, will transmit the ads to audiences of predetermined age, income level, taste, and life-style.

Big companies employ both an in-house advertising staff and an outside agency. The agency people usually create the campaign and produce the print and television ads with the approval of the in-house staff. Since most large advertising agencies are centered in New York, Chicago, and Los Angeles, most creative jobs in the field are clustered in these cities. Jobs in corporate departments as well as in newspapers and television and radio stations are available throughout the country.

Starting salaries (for space and time buyers, junior copywriters, and market researchers) range from $10,000 to $12,000. The salaries of top executives, especially those who own their own agencies, are legendary. The average executive salary is $45,300, and with profit sharing and perks the annual take can be much higher. In general, salaries of advertising managers associated with corporations are higher for work done with consumer products companies than they are for work done with industrial products firms.

No single path to this glamour industry is preferred. Job experience may be even more important in gaining a foothold than a college degree in advertising or marketing. Most important are talent, imagination, and determination, since many more people are attracted to the industry than it can possibly absorb. A certain independence is also useful, since accounts switch and advertising revenues vary, making this one of the least secure of job markets.

ARCHITECTS

Some artists are spiritual and dreamy, but some are practical, technical, and result-oriented. Those in the second category make good architects. Architects may design houses, entire towns, redevelopment of existing cities, shopping centers, churches, and many structures in between.

A client knows what is needed and how much can be paid. The architect draws up a rough plan of how it could be done. Once accepted, the plans become more precise, with exact dimensions, perhaps even a scale model. After any modifications have been made, the architect and client contact the builder and specify the construction materials and due date. Then the architect periodically checks the progress until it is finished.

All states require an architect to be licensed. To qualify for the exam, applicants must have either a Bachelor of Architecture degree with three years of experience in an architect's office; a Master of Architecture degree with two years of experience; or twelve years of experience and a passing grade on a qualifying test. Of the 101 schools giving degrees in architecture 80 have been accredited by the National Architectural Accrediting

Board. It takes five years to earn a bachelor's degree in architecture and six to earn a master's.

The first job out of school for an architect is usually as a junior drafter under a licensed architect in a firm. After a few years, it's possible to move up to a position of chief drafter, designer, or supervisor, particularly if the young architect has become licensed in that time.

Architects working for the federal government earn an average of $25,000. Salaries in private practice are considerably higher, ranging in the vicinity of $40,000.

ART DIRECTORS

That elegant glass of bubbling golden champagne that looks real enough to drink, that cigarette carton hovering refreshingly near a crisp waterfall, the sexy woman whose hair is carefully blown to look just carefree enough are all distinctive images constructed with great precision according to the creative vision of a commercial art director. The highly imaginative mind behind the scenes who is responsible for the look of most of America's print media is the head of a production art team. Some art directors work hard to maintain the stylistic uniqueness of a magazine like *Cosmopolitan* or *The New Yorker,* while others develop the look of new ads to go in a newspaper or on a billboard. Increasingly, these commercial artists are also designing visual graphics for television and for store packaging and window displays.

In publishing companies, advertising agencies, textile firms, television studios, and department stores, art directors supervise a team of commercial artists. Once they have come up with an idea they work with illustrators, layout artists, photographers, letterers, and mechanical artists to produce the complete design. The art director is responsible for getting all of the parts together and for getting the final product exactly right. This can often be nerve-racking under the pressure of publishing deadlines.

Most art directors rise to their positions from the ranks of commercial artists. They need a strong background in art as well as experience with photography, typography, and printing production methods within the business world. Early educational training may be in a two- or four-year trade school, junior college, or four-year college. Once out in the field, new jobs depend on a good portfolio and a strong reputation. Competition for these jobs is tough, and the few openings will tend to be in the areas of visual graphics and industrial design. Art directors earn between $500 and $600 or more a week.

ARTISTS (COMMERCIAL)

Commercial artists carry out the concepts developed by the art director. Depending on the size of the agency or company, the art work may require a specialist for each stage, or may be done with a few people with combined talents. The first step for a commercial artist is to render a rough sketch of the ad, called a comp. At this point, the layout person arranges the pictures and copy for the typographer. Lettering must be done by choosing the appropriate typeface and size for headlines. Finally, the paste-up and mechanicals are made by pasting the finished copy and pictures onto cardboard for the engraver.

Art trade school graduates and college grads who have majored in art usually start as trainees in agencies by assisting the art director. In this way they can develop skills while on the job.

A free-lance artist will do quick, slick jobs when an agency runs short of time or staff. The finished product is photocopied for the artist's portfolio. These free-lancers may be on salary elsewhere, at least until they can get top dollar from several regular accounts.

Salaried commercial artists and art directors work a thirty-five-hour week, with some high-pressure overtime for special rush jobs. Job prospects are better for free-lancers and mechanical artists than they are for art directors and layout specialists. The wider variety of expertise, the better. Illustrators and commercial artists earn an average $250 per week, or more, depending on the demand for their particular talents. Creative artists in top advertising agencies earn between $400 and $500 per week.

BROADCAST TECHNICIANS

The men and women behind the scenes who make it possible to see the national news in Wichita and to hear the Berlin

Philharmonic live from Tokyo are the broadcast technicians of television and radio. Also referred to as engineers, the communications technicians handle sound and lighting equipment, video cameras and recorders, broadcast transmitters, and other electronic equipment used to create and transmit radio and television programs.

In small stations one person may have to be a jack-of-all-trades, whereas in larger stations that do more production, particularly in New York, Los Angeles, and Washington, D.C., the jobs are more highly specialized. In nearly all cases, however, these positions include both studio and location work.

Broadcasting in the United States is regulated by the Federal Communications Commission (FCC), and all broadcasters must pass a written test to obtain either a First Class Radiotelephone Operator's License or a Third Class Operator License. Science and electronics courses are useful background; technical schools and colleges give special courses designed to teach what you need to know to obtain a license. In addition, a college degree in engineering would enable one to move into the higher positions in this field.

There are 22,500 broadcast technicians who work at all hours of the day and night to keep up the electronic flow of information. Beginners earn between $155 and $215; experienced workers earn $200 to $450. Television pays more than radio, and large stations in big cities usually have higher pay scales than those in smaller towns.

DANCERS—MODERN AND BALLET

Perhaps the single most demanding discipline in the performing arts is dancing, one of the most difficult occupations to pursue. Of the eight thousand professional dancers (both classical and modern), at any given moment probably half of them are unemployed. Even though a dancer may be out of work, dance demands constant practice and rugged rehearsals. The professional life of a dancer is relatively short, spanning no more than two decades, though there are numerous exceptions to this rule.

The minimum wage for work in a stage production is $250 per week plus an allowance of $30 a day when on the road. Solo performers routinely command at least twice the basic salary.

Television and movie performances can supplement these wages, but the duration of such work is rather brief.

Employers contribute to health and welfare funds of the various unions and guilds that represent dancers. Fringe benefits are not exceptional, and many dancers have to rely on unemployment insurance and welfare benefits to make ends meet.

The growing popularity of dance in urban areas has created new employment opportunities for dancers. Moreover, the health and exercise field has opened up new opportunities to teach dance. Indeed, teaching is often the second stage of a professional dancer's career.

EDITORS (BOOK PUBLISHING)

With forty thousand books published every year in this country, there are nevertheless few employment opportunities for editors. However, the glamour of publishing has lured any number of English majors, would-be writers, journalists, educators, and liberal arts graduates to the field. Certainly a varied background helps in the trade department, since editors must deal with a broad diversity of ideas and subject matter.

Many editors start their careers as readers, evaluating manuscripts for senior editors and winnowing the "slush piles"—the unsolicited manuscripts that come in over the transom. Editors must have not only technical editing skills and a command of the English language but also an instinct for markets. Commercial publishers survive by the quality of their list of books, and that is the direct responsibility of the house's acquisitions editors. Acquiring potentially successful literary properties is one of the main jobs of an editor, and eating the required publisher's lunch is one of the pleasant perquisites.

Besides possessing a love of words, editors must also be able to compose critiques, abstract the main themes of a work, and write convincing promotional material for the sales department. For these talents, editors are paid rather frugally, with starting salaries in the vicinity of $12,000. Senior editors earn $25,000 to $30,000, depending on their past successes and stable of authors. Chances for advancement are reasonable, not because the industry is growing rapidly, but due to a perpetual game of musical chairs at most publishing houses; tenure, to put it mildly, is tenuous. Though New York is the center of the communications and publishing industries, Los Angeles, Chicago, Washington, D.C., and Boston all have healthy magazine and publishing businesses.

FLORAL DESIGNERS

Florists may well have one of the most appealing work places: they are surrounded by the perfume of flowers and blooming plants. For the thirty-seven thousand floral designers, their shops may not be the Elysian Fields, but they do provide a pleasant leafy retreat compared to some other forms of commerce. Florists need no formal training, but must have a flair for flower arrangement, a green thumb, and the ability to manage a retail establishment.

While there is no foreseeable growth in demand for floral designers, there is a healthy increase in the number of plants and trees that are finding their way into American homes. Floral designers working for retail shops are paid between $3.50 and $7.00 per hour. However, fringe benefits are likely to be minimal since most florists are small shopkeepers with limited resources.

INDUSTRIAL DESIGNERS

Industrial designers work with manufacturers and corporations to make products both more efficient and more marketable. Essentially trained as artists with skills in construction, form, and style, industrial designers also need to call upon knowledge in the areas of engineering and marketing as they develop an overall image for the item they are trying to sell. Most of the country's twelve thousand industrial designers work for large companies that make consumer or industrial goods. Others work for design consulting firms or work independently as free-lancers.

Industrial designers complete a course of study at the college level whether it be in an art school, a technical college, or a university. Programs at the different institutions vary, with some placing more emphasis on a range of academic subjects while others focus on studio, lab, and machining courses.

Starting salaries in this field range from $10,000 to $14,000, moving up to $15,000 to $20,000 with experience. An industrial designer with great creativity and skill may earn more than $25,000 depending upon his/her clients or employer.

INTERIOR DECORATORS

A majority of the nation's thirty-seven thousand interior decorators work for large retailers of furniture and home accessories. Their salaries are commensurate with the sales personnel since their function is similar—suggesting the components of interiors. A minority of interior decorators work independently, selling their own ideas for a consultant's fee or receiving a commission from the retailer for the client's purchases.

To work for an architectural firm, large retailer, or department store, one needs training in either a professional school or a college for a period of three or four years. Starting salaries begin in the range of $150 per week, and employed interior decorators average up to $13,000 a year plus the possibility of sales commissions. Self-employed interior decorators can, when quite successful, earn $50,000 to $100,000 a year from consultations.

INTERPRETERS

Oru naalum ungakallai marravaen. If you don't speak the South Indian language Tamil, you'll need an interpreter to tell you this means "I shall never forget you." Interpreters translate from one language to another, and although many Americans are bilingual and go through this process all of the time, there are only 175 people working full-time as interpreters in the United States. Many of them work in New York for the United Nations, while most of the others work in Washington, D.C., for a variety of international and federal agencies.

Interpreters must have a "feel" for language and appreciate cultural distinctions and subtleties. One United Nations meeting broke up in gales of laughter when a delegate was making a serious point. "How," he asked, "could you explain this to the man in the street?" Over the earphones came the interpreter's rendition: "And how, sir, can you explain this to a streetwalker?"

Professional interpreters are fluent in at least two languages and often in three or four. Two schools in the country offer special programs in this field, Georgetown University and Monterey Institute of Foreign Studies. They provide courses that specifically prepare students for the complexities of conference interpretation and translation. A university degree is recommended but not essential in all areas of interpreting work. The

Immigration Department, for example, has hired people whose background and linguistic ability allow them to translate rapidly at a meeting. A talented interpreter must be able to translate both simultaneously and consecutively.

The salaries of interpreters vary with the type of interpreting. The United Nations pays $14,300 tax free for a starting salary, while an experienced interpreter there earns $30,000. Junior interpreters in the U.S. Department of State earn an average of $17,000, and free-lance conference interpreters are paid from $125 to $160 a day.

LANDSCAPE ARCHITECTS

We often think of landscape architects as the designers who draft plans for a new park or who decide where to plant trees in a new shopping mall. But as environmental planning becomes increasingly important in building, landscape architects are beginning to take on a variety of new tasks: planning and designing transportation systems, construction of housing developments on landfill, the safety of industrial growth, and disposition of wastes.

In thirty-eight states landscape architects must pass a national test in order to practice. Candidates applying to take the exam usually have a B.A. in landscape architecture as well as a few years of experience in the field. In some cases a long apprenticeship (six to eight years) can replace the B.A. requirement.

Most landscape architects work for themselves. Others work for architectural or engineering firms or for government agencies involved with urban planning, forest management, highways, or parks.

A beginning landscape architect earns between $10,500 and $12,500, while those with experience generally earn between $15,000 and $20,000 a year. Landscape architects with high levels of creativity and skill may earn over $30,000 a year, particularly if they have their own firms.

MUSICIANS

There are 127,000 musicians in America, including Vladimir Horowitz, Pearl Bailey, the Chicago Symphony Orchestra, the United States Marine Band, the Lounge Lizards, X-ray Specs, nervus Rex, Pandemonium, and your local piano teacher.

Whether your preference is Puccini or punk (and few musicians play both), discipline and willingness to put in hours of rehearsal are as important as natural talent. Training should start early. Private lessons are available from experienced musicians in most cities, and hundreds of colleges, universities, and music conservatories offer degrees in instrumental and vocal music, as well as in music education.

As might be expected, a saxophone player and a church organist work different hours for different wages. Most members of symphony orchestras have master wage agreements that guarantee them fifty to fifty-two weeks of work a year. Other musicians may have a long wait between gigs. For this reason, many talented instrumentalists opt for teaching, either instead of or in addition to performing and recording.

For those who choose to perform, it is smart to seek work in those cities where most entertainment and recording activities are centered: New York, Chicago, Los Angeles, Nashville, Miami Beach, and New Orleans. Classical musicians of high caliber may seek a chair in any of the thirty-one major symphony orchestras, seventy-six metropolitan orchestras, and hundreds of community orchestras throughout the country. The armed forces also have many different musical organizations offering employment.

Major symphony orchestras pay minimum salaries of $200 to $400 per week, the variation largely a factor of geography. For instance, the Metropolitan Opera orchestra members are paid $525 per week for a sixteen-hour week. Metropolitan symphonies pay $20 to $40 per concert. Musicians in big-city show business bands, playing dances, club dates, musical comedies, industrial shows, and the like earn $40 to $53 for three hours of work. Musicians who perform for recorded sound tracks for motion pictures get $93 for a three-hour session; those who do television commercials, $48 for one hour. The minimum for a phonograph recording session is three hours at $110. Of course, the stars make much more and have a greater choice of when, where, and for whom they will perform.

In the near future, jobs that provide stable, year-round employment will be hardest to find and competition for all performance and teaching opportunities will be keen. There will, however, continue to be a great need for outstanding players of stringed instruments, and for topflight, experienced accompanists.

NEWSPAPER REPORTERS

Contrary to popular belief, the newspaper business is alive and healthy with 1,762 daily newspapers and 7,579 weekly newspapers employing forty-five thousand reporters. As a component of the communications and publishing industry, the newspaper business provides a number of economic advantages for journalists. Not only are newspapers in reasonable condition, but journalists have easy access to affiliated fields, from broadcasting to public relations. However, the fly in the ointment is overproduction: journalism schools are turning out record numbers of graduates, fourteen thousand a year with various degrees. So while employment prospects are good in the trade, competition for jobs is intense.

Starting salaries for reporters average $10,600 under contracts negotiated by the Newspaper Guild. Salaries depend on the size of the paper as well as years of seniority. Average guild salaries after four or five years experience are $19,240, but small papers pay as little as $10,000 while large metropolitan ones pay in excess of $26,000. The major wire services pay their employees approximately $20,000 per year.

PHOTOGRAPHERS

Of the nation's eighty-five thousand photographers, a third are in business for themselves. From passport snapshots to aerial landscapes, photography continues to be one of the great growth industries of the twentieth century with varied application in industry, law enforcement, advertising, government, science, and the arts. While there are dozens of schools giving photographic degrees, and diplomas and formal training may be helpful in beginning a career, it is rarely a necessity unless one wishes to teach.

News "fotogs" with Newspaper Guild newspapers start work earning between $175 and $225 a week, but after four or five years of experience they earn an average of $320 per week. Top news photographers earn $500 a week. In government service, photographers start at between $8,320 and $11,520, with experienced ones earning as much as $18,460 a year.

Since the capital outlays for free-lance photographers are not great, there is considerable appeal for independents to run their own shops. The erratic earnings tend to be offset by substantial fees for successful photographers. Free-lance photojournalism and fashion or industrial photography are highly competitive professions and demand a resilient and persistent spirit. But those few who do become stars can earn between $750 and $1,800 per day shooting models or microchips for fashion magazines or annual reports.

RADIO AND TELEVISION BROADCASTING

During the 1980s, over-the-air broadcasting will be supplemented—and to some degree supplanted—by the "new media." Cable television, direct satellite-to-home transmission, cassette and videodisc players, subscription and pay TV have been hovering on the horizon for years. Now they are gathering the "critical mass" of audience necessary to warrant the production of new programming.

How different this programming will be from today's menu of sitcoms, entertainment specials, movies, sports, and news is impossible to predict. But the new media do promise the possibility of special interest material. Many new jobs will be created by this new technology. Most of them will be in programming and production, and many will be outside the present broadcasting establishment, although the networks are rapidly moving into cable and busily stockpiling shows for the home video market.

Meanwhile, most of the jobs in television and radio today are at local broadcasting stations. Of the 160,000 full-time and 40,000 part-time workers, about 60 percent work in commercial radio and 40 percent in commercial television. Several thousand more employees work for independent producers, making programs and commercials. About 1,000 people work for the seven national radio networks and 14,000 for the three major television networks. Public broadcasting (local and national, radio and television) accounts for 9,000 full-time and 4,000 part-time jobs. The nearly equal number of jobs in radio and television takes on different meaning when you realize that there are 7,650 commercial radio stations compared with only 730 television stations in the country.

Some small radio stations are literally mom-and-pop operations; many are run by four or five people—an engineer, an announcer, and maybe a station manager who doubles as sales representative. In these cases, programming is a very simple matter of reading news-wire copy, playing records, and plugging in network shows. At the opposite end, a big city television station may employ hundreds of people in several departments: engineering, sales, general administration, programming, and production.

The history of the movie industry and the news media has dictated a geographical split in network television program production. The capital of film- and tape-oriented dramatic programming is in Hollywood, and the live news and public affairs center is New York. Jobs outside these two cities are almost totally confined to local stations' news and public affairs coverage.

The trends toward the use of new broadcast and communication media like cable TV, video cassettes, and videodiscs will expand job opportunities for independent producers, especially those already established as suppliers to commercial television. It will not create jobs for engineers and technical personnel (already a declining job market), since the modes of interconnection will be provided by satellite and other common carriers. Furthermore, technical jobs within cable and broadcast stations will be eroded by automated systems.

There are many different kinds of jobs, along with a wide range of salaries, available in radio and television broadcasting. They range from the $1 million a year paid for anchorwoman Barbara Walters, and $500,000 for a prominent weather announcer, to the $6.56 an hour earned by the average nonsupervisory broadcast worker.

Not surprisingly, salaries for producers in the network news and public affairs departments are higher than for independent stations outside the major metropolitan areas. The average producer's salary is about $50,000, with a range between $45,000 and $70,000. Executive producers of news and documentary programs earn between $65,000 and $350,000, but it has been estimated that no more than 10 percent of all network news producers make over $60,000.

Clerks, secretaries, and production assistants, with salary ranges of $140 to $170 per week at the networks, subsist on the glory of it all, or more likely, the overtime. Middle management jobs in broadcasting are comparable in pay to other white collar institutions. It is only at the senior management level and in the rarefied atmosphere of the star system that agents and lawyers negotiate six-figure salaries.

SINGERS

Singing is a vibration of the vocal cords that produces a musical sound, pleasant or unpleasant, depending on the training and natural gifts of the singer. About twenty-three thousand Americans sing well enough to get paid for it, and many others who do not choose to perform teach singing or conduct choruses in schools, conservatories, and universities.

Although a naturally good voice will become apparent early, training should not begin until adolescence. Piano lessons can start much earlier and will help the singer become familiar with music theory and composition. Vocal training is essential for those who aspire to a classical repertoire, but not absolutely necessary for popular music performance, which depends upon microphones for projection and does not generally demand the range, diction, and delivery necessary for operatic or other classical scores.

Although singing jobs, especially short-term engagements in opera, concerts, movies, theaters, and nightclubs, will be plentiful in the coming decades, there will not be enough of them to provide steady employment for all qualified singers. Also, like dancers, football players, and models, singers must be aware that their careers may be relatively short, as age takes its toll.

Wages vary. A prima donna with the Met earns thousands of dollars per performance: Joan Sutherland has earned $25,000 for a one-night stand. And one golden record can provide a comfortable income for life. However, the standard fee for a solo concert performance is $200, and singers in the Metropolitan Opera chorus are paid $409 a week. The pay for singers in television is around $150 for a one-hour show.

WRITERS (FREE-LANCE—BOOKS)

With all the books that are published every year, a surprisingly small percentage are produced by free-lance writers. Indeed, most books are written by people in their respective trades: a microbiologist on the mysteries of fungi; a surgeon on the economics of bypass operations; a Hollywood celebrity on early alcoholic addiction; an apologia from an ex-politico.

Nonfiction is the meat and potatoes of the writing business, while fiction is the dessert. Publishers' advances for the latter may range from a couple of thousand dollars to a recent record-breaking $3.2 million for the paperback rights to Judith Krantz's *Princess Daisy.* Advances for nonfiction range from nothing, as in the case of medical textbooks, to substantial five- and six-figure sums for original and salable works.

The large and enticing advances aside, book publishing is not a lucrative business. A study by the writers' organization P.E.N. found that the median income of its members was $4,700, with 68 percent making less than $10,000 and 9 percent earning nothing, or rather earning a living at something other than writing. Agents traditionally receive 10 percent of an author's earnings, although some, like Scott Meredith, take 15 percent. While most writers are represented by agents, some are not: Edmund Wilson, the essayist, had no use for them and did very well.

A report by the Authors Guild, based on a series of surveys to its members in the seventies, found that 6 percent of all book contracts paid no advance, 30 percent were under $5,000, 25 percent were between $5,000 and $9,999, 18 percent were between $10,000 and $19,999, and 21 percent earned advances over $20,000.

WRITERS—TECHNICAL

Most writers are employed by communications companies—newspapers, magazines, radio, television (see "Newspaper Reporters," page 194, and "Radio and Television Broadcasting," page 195)—and by industrial corporations as technical writers. There are over twenty-two thousand technical writers specializing in electronics, aerospace, and consumer industries where they communicate scientific and technical information. By preparing manuals and instructional materials, technical writers attempt to explain to the lay public the intricacies of our futuristic society. It helps to have a Bachelor of Science and a minor in English to become an accomplished technical writer, but there are no consistent formal requirements. Salaries for technical writers range from $12,500 to $24,000 a year, in addition to free-lance assignments that pay anywhere from $100 to $500 per article.

26

If you do not think about the future,
you cannot have one.
—JOHN GALSWORTHY, *Swansong*

PROGNOSIS FOR THE EIGHTIES

JOBS WITH THE MOST OPENINGS, 1980–90

What can we expect in the way of job availability for the 1980s? Will the glut of medical, law, and business school graduates make it impossible to get a job in those professions? Based on assessments of replacement needs and growth, the occupations listed below are projected to offer the largest numbers of openings in the next few years. Competition for openings will vary by occupation.

Accountants
Assemblers
Bank clerks
Blue-collar worker supervisors
Bookkeepers
Building custodians
Carpenters
Cashiers
Construction laborers
Cooks and chefs
Engineers

Guards
Industrial machinery repairers
Kindergarten and elementary school teachers
Licensed practical nurses
Local truck drivers
Nursing aides, orderlies, and attendants
Private household workers
Real estate agents and brokers
Receptionists
Registered nurses
Retail sales workers
Secretaries and stenographers
Typists
Waiters and waitresses
Wholesale trade sales workers

FASTEST GROWING JOBS, 1980–90

For the following occupations, employment in 1990 is projected to be at least 50 percent higher than it was in 1978.

Bank clerks
Bank officers and financial managers
Business machine repairers
City managers
Computer service technicians
Construction inspectors
Dental assistants
Dental hygienists
Dining room attendants and dishwashers
Flight attendants
Guards
Health service administrators
Homemaker–home health aides
Industrial machinery repairers
Landscape architects
Licensed practical nurses
Lithographers
Nursing aides, orderlies, and attendants
Occupational therapists

Occupational therapy assistants
Physical therapists
Podiatrists
Respiratory therapy workers
Speech pathologists and audiologists
Teacher aides
Travel agents

INDEX